Budgeting Public Funds

Budgeting Public Funds

The Decision Process in an Urban School District

Donald Gerwin

The University of Wisconsin Press
Madison, Milwaukee, and London
1969

Published by
The University of Wisconsin Press
Box 1379, Madison, Wisconsin 53701

The University of Wisconsin Press, Ltd.
27-29 Whitfield Street, London, W.1

Standard Book Number 299-05270-2
Library of Congress Catalog Card
Number 69-17326

To M. G., S. G., and L. G.

Acknowledgments

I am indebted to a number of people without whose help this work could not have been written. Professor Otto Davis, the chairman of my thesis committee, was instrumental in bringing my ideas to an operational state. My appreciation also goes to the remaining members of the committee, Professors Richard Cyert, Herbert Simon, and Andrew Stedry, for their assistance. Of the numerous other individuals who made comments on various portions of the manuscript Professor Chadwick Haberstroh must be singled out for his help. I am also grateful to B. Pesek, G. P. E. Clarkson, M. Lurie, T. Mahoney, T. R. Rao, P. Soelberg, and C. E. Weber.

Mr. and Mrs. Leland Hazard were responsible for introducing me to the former superintendent of the Pittsburgh schools, Dr. Sidney P. Marland. Dr. Marland must be acknowledged not only for the time he devoted, but also for his foresight in cooperating with a study that offered little in immediate, tangible returns. There are literally scores of individuals in the Pittsburgh school system who devoted their time to answering my questions. In particular, I would like to single out Mr. Regis Sloan, Chief Accountant (retired) and Mr. Clifton Mellinger, Associate Superintendent of Business (deceased). Mr. William Jones and Miss Dorothy Fafata of the accounting department were also very helpful.

I wish to thank *Administrative Science Quarterly* for permission to use material from "Towards a Theory of Public Budgetary De-

Making"; *Industrial Relations* for "Compensation Decisions ublic Organizations"; *Management Science* for "A Process odel of Budgeting in a Public School System"; and the Research Division of the National Education Association for allowing me to use data from a number of their published reports.

This research was sponsored at various times by Resources for the Future, Inc.; The Graduate School of Industrial Administration, Carnegie-Mellon University; The Division of Organizational Sciences, Case Institute of Technology (now School of Management, Case-Western Reserve University); and the School of Business Administration, the University of Wisconsin—Milwaukee.

Various stages of the manuscript were typed by Nancy Henke and Barbara Leach.

Finally, my wife Marlene must be thanked for the many hours she spent proofreading and collecting data, as well as for her advice and understanding while the job was being done.

D. G.

Milwaukee, Wisconsin
September 1, 1968

Contents

List of Tables

List of Illustrations
and Flow Charts

Figure

Chart

Budgeting Public Funds

1
Introduction

Scholars in economics, political science, and administration have been concerned for many years with the study of both how public funds should be allocated and how public budgeting decisions actually are made. Yet little agreement has emerged concerning the outlines of a theory for either of these areas. This study will explore the second area, the decision-making process, by taking a rather unconventional approach which utilizes newly developed techniques in administrative theory. Such an approach, it is believed, will result in a better understanding of public resource allocation.

This understanding should in turn provide valuable insights into the ways and means of budgetary decision-making. It should aid, first of all, in determining the value of practices currently used to distribute funds. An administrator, for example, may base next year's decisions on this year's budget not because he is unaware of the advantages of reviewing his entire program, but in order to reduce his decision-making to manageable proportions. Understanding should also promote the development of effective budgeting procedures. Suppose it is found that an administrator shuns long-range forecasts because of their inaccuracy. A new method of allocation that depends upon the use of such forecasts should not be recommended unless he could at the same time be supplied with more sophisticated forecasting techniques. Furthermore, understanding should lead to the ability to predict future patterns of resource allocation in a more reliable manner than can be done by the projection of trends. Needless to say, prediction facilitates planning since it yields knowledge of such adverse conditions as impending deficits before they arise. Finally, when the ways in which a certain variable influences the distribution of resources are known, the effects of hypothetical changes in its value can be determined. If it is an externally determined variable, such as a state regulation, the administrator should then be able to decide whether or not to press for the change. If it is internally controllable, as in the case of a new administrative policy, he should be better able to determine whether or not to put it into effect.

Characteristics of the Study

This discussion of public resource allocation is devoted to a study of the manner in which the operating (general fund) budget is compiled. Typically, this set of decisions has been viewed as arising from an intricate web of economic, political, and institutional variables. Accordingly, it has not usually been considered amenable to scientific analysis. In order to deal effectively with the complex nature of the problem, the following strategy has been adopted.

An analysis of the decision process has been the focus of attention, first of all, because it is felt that it will provide deeper insights into budgeting than more conventional methods.[1] The public administrator is assumed to encounter a large number of environmental stimuli when he prepares his budget, including the demands of employees for higher wages, requests by property holders to keep taxes down, and the availability of higher-level governmental funds for certain activities. He becomes aware of their existence by analyzing information from written reports, conversations, personal observation, budgetary requests, and so forth. Because many

[1] My particular approach is characteristic of James G. March and Herbert A. Simon in *Organizations* (New York: John Wiley, 1958); and Richard M. Cyert and James G. March in *A Behavioral Theory of the Firm* (Englewood Cliffs, N.J.: Prentice-Hall, 1963).

stimuli recur each year, the administrator over time develops a fairly stable collection of responses to them in the form of standard decision rules. The appropriate set of rules is called into service at the correct time if an adequate flow of information is maintained.

This approach focuses attention on two aspects of the decision process in particular: the types of information gathered when the budget is being prepared and the rules used in making choices. The fact that formal rules are an essential ingredient of bureaucratic decision-making is well established. Their importance has been discussed by Max Weber, who developed the classical theory of bureaucracy, as well as by such recent writers as Anthony Downs.[2] Whether in fact unwritten rules are used in the specific area of public budgeting has not been extensively investigated. This discussion has so far implied that such rules should most readily be found where the organization has been frequently exposed to a particular stimulus, but that where new stimuli are making their presence felt, intuition will play the major role. It is my contention that public budgeting is more typical of the former situation than the latter; this point will be defended in the following chapters by the presentation of allocation rules and evidence to support their existence.

The second characteristic of this study, the development of a computer simulation model, follows directly from the first. Once the decision rules used in budget preparation are discovered, they can be recorded in the form of flow diagrams; that is, in the sequence in which they are applied. The information in the flow diagrams can then be translated into a suitable computer programming language and punched onto cards. The result will be a formal model capable of predicting allocation decisions [3]

[2] Max Weber, *The Theory of Social and Economic Organization,* 1st ed. (New York: Oxford University Press, 1947), pp. 329–341; and Anthony Downs, *Inside Bureaucracy* (Boston: Little, Brown and Co., 1967), pp. 59–61.

[3] Geoffrey P. E. Clarkson in *Portfolio Selection: A Simulation of Trust Investment* (Englewood Cliffs, N.J.: Prentice-Hall, 1962), uses similar methodology to explain how a trust investment officer selected stocks for his clients' portfolios.

This unconventional approach has been selected for several reasons. It allows, first of all, a relatively precise formulation of ideas, making the task of finding contradictions easier and clearly highlighting areas in which not enough research has been done. It also provides an opportunity to test these ideas empirically, since the model's predictions can be compared to actual past decisions.

In addition, a formal simulation model has benefits for the public administrator. It can relieve him of the burden of making innumerable routine decisions and give him more time to concentrate on crucial ones. By providing an inventory of the organization's present strategies for allocating resources, it facilitates the transfer of knowledge to new administrators and serves as a guide in solving recurring problems, such as the need to eliminate deficits. More important, rigorous formulation opens the possibility of examining the effects of changes in policy and environmental conditions on the budget. Specifically, the changes in the allocation of funds brought about by altering the parameters of the model can be observed.[4] An important advantage is that this can be done for more than merely one year ahead. Most public organizations find it extremely difficult at present to make calculations beyond the coming year, even though they must make decisions involving long-term commitments of funds. Some illustrations of using a model of the budgetary process as a planning aid are given in Chapter 6.

A third characteristic of this study is that it will deal exclusively with a single public organization: the Pittsburgh school system. In part, the time required to analyze the process—since it involves a whole set of interrelated decisions—precludes a more comprehensive study. A general model would also have a great deal of difficulty in coping with the diverse legal regulations to which districts even in the same state are subject. It seems more realistic, given our present limited understanding of how fiscal dependence,

[4] This suggestion is analogous to the method used by Charles P. Bonini in *Simulation of Information and Decision Systems in the Firm* (Englewood Cliffs, N.J.: Prentice-Hall, 1963), for an analysis of a hypothetical business firm.

state maximums on tax levies, the methods of selecting school board members, and other such variables influence the budgetary process, to be content with less sweeping objectives.

These remarks should not be taken to suggest that I am uninterested in the generality of my findings. On the contrary, one of my main arguments is that studying the decision process in one organization serves as an excellent basis for the development of a more general theory which can be tested at a later time. Consequently, the extent to which the model's school district is representative of other large city school districts will be examined in Chapter 2 and a set of hypotheses meant to apply to more than a single organization will be developed in Chapter 8.

2
Background and Overview

In order to evaluate the risks encountered in generalizing from a single organization, the main similarities and differences between the model's district and other large school systems need to be pointed out. In addition, the budget and its rearrangement require explanation in order to emphasize the decisions of major concern, while an examination of the budgetary process and an outline of the model's version of the process will provide an integrating framework for the succeeding chapters. A brief discussion of the formal organization of the school system is also of importance, since it will provide a background for the selection in Chapter 3 of the subunits to be analyzed on an individual basis.

A Comparison of the Model's School District with Other Large School Systems

One of the major problems facing any study of a single organization is the extent to which its conclusions can be generalized. Perhaps the best way of overcoming that difficulty in this study is by establishing whether or not the school system is typical of the other large city school districts in the nation. Comparisons involving about 150 systems will therefore be made along the dimensions of size, financial characteristics, and legal regulations. In all cases, the National Education Association's definition of "large" enrollment as being 25,000 students or more will be used, since most of the data are taken from that source.[1] Because of problems encountered in compiling information, the same year could not be used for every category, but an effort was made to keep as close as possible to the 1965/66 school year because the last district budget studied was for 1965. A summary of the findings appears in Table 1.

The model's district is located in a city with a population of slightly over 600,000 (according to the 1960 census). Its elementary and secondary day school enrollment is 77,789, which is virtually at the mean for large systems.[2] The total number of full-time classroom teachers is 2,768, which is also near average when the range is considered.[3] A measure of revenue composition, the percentage of receipts from local sources, is a little above the mean, but again not significantly when the range is taken into account.[4] The district's effective property tax rate, arrived at by multiplying the reported rate and the reported estimated ratio of assessed to market value,[5] is also apparently close to the average.[6] Current spending represents all costs of operating elementary and secondary day schools except for capital outlay, debt service, and federally funded projects. The system's figure of $34,707,478 is very near the mean.[7] A comparison of current spending per pupil in average daily membership yields a similar result considering the range.[8]

[1] Some districts at the lower limit of enrollment are Riverside, Calif.; Hartford, Conn.; Pueblo, Colo.; Topeka, Kan.; Providence, R.I.; Hampton, Va.; and Racine, Wis.

[2] National Education Association, Research Division, *Selected Statistics of Local School Systems 1965/66* (Research Report 1967–R15; Washington, D.C.: The Association, 1967), pp. 8, 31.

[3] *Ibid.*, pp. 10, 39.

[4] *Ibid.*, pp. 12, 48.

[5] The resulting figure is the tax per $1,000 which would be required to produce the same amount of revenue as the reported rate if property was assessed at full market value.

[6] NEA, *Selected Statistics,* pp. 15, 48.

[7] *Ibid.*, pp. 16, 56. The mean value is positively biased since some districts unavoidably included federally financed projects in their current spending.

[8] *Ibid.*, pp. 18, 56. The mean value is positively biased for the same reason as in footnote 7.

Table 1—Size, Financial, and Legal Characteristics of Large School Systems[a]

Size and financial characteristics	The model's system	Mean of large systems	Range for large systems	Number reporting	Year
Enrollment	77,789	76,684	25,005 – 1,065,909	149/156	1965/66
Number of teachers	2,768	3,025	874 – 51,491	149/156	1965/66
Local revenue share	63%	56%	18.7% – 92.8%[b]	149/156	1965/66
Effective tax rate	$9.35	$10.20	$1.05 – $27.45	145/156	1965/66
Current spending	$34,707,478	$36,624,100	$7,967,450 – $820,050,799	149/156	1965/66
Spending per pupil	$455.43	$484.01	$238.40 – $780.82	149/156	1965/66

Legal characteristics	The model's system	Number of similar large systems	Number reporting	Year
Fiscal independence	Yes	102	148/156	1965/66
Biennial legislative decisions affecting budgets	Yes	$\geq$ 82	149/156	1965
Board appointed	Yes	37	159/159	1966/67
"Effective" state limit on property tax	Yes	44	107/121	1959/60

[a]The data for this table were taken from the sources cited in footnotes 2–4, 6–10, and 12–15 for this chapter.
[b]Excludes Hawaii and District of Columbia because their state-local organizations are not comparable with other systems.

Indeed, it appears that the system is near average in regard to every size and financial characteristic examined—an indication that the generality of the conclusions reached in this study cannot be easily contested on these grounds. On the other hand, the wide ranges in the characteristics' values indicate that it would be difficult to find a typical school system. At the very least, caution must be exercised in applying any conclusions to districts at either extreme.

The legal framework within which the district operates is less consistent with other school systems'. As shown in Table 1, fiscal independence and biennial financial decisions by the state legislature affecting local districts' budgets are typical of at least a majority of other large city school districts, but an appointed school board and the state's power to limit the property tax rate are not. A fiscally independent school system is one which has the power to levy its own taxes. Since these districts do not have to rely on any other governmental body to raise revenues (although they may be subject to maximum tax rate limitations), they have fewer constraints to deal with when preparing their budgets. The model's district and most others are fiscally independent.[9]

It is also important to consider whether a state legislature makes annual or biennial financial decisions affecting its school districts' budgets, since in the latter case the districts may be forced to develop a two-year planning horizon. There can be no doubt when such decisions are made, provided a state legislature meets on a one or two-year basis. Some states, however, hold annual sessions in which laws affecting the state's budget can be passed in any year, but other laws only in alternate years.[10] For these states it is not clear whether decisions affecting local districts' budgets are made every year or every other year. Pennsylvania's legislature met in odd years until 1959, but then moved into this third category. In those even years after 1959 which were considered part of this

[9] *Ibid.,* pp. 26, 85.
[10] Council of State Governments, *The Book of the States, 1966–1967,* vol. 16 (Chicago: The Council, 1966), pp. 46–47.

study (1960, 1962, 1964), however, it was not legally possible
to enact laws changing school district taxes, tax rates, and the state
reimbursement formula.[11] Thus, for all practical purposes, the
state legislature has met biennially to make decisions which affect
the budgets of its local districts. A true annual session was adopted
in Pennsylvania in 1967.

In Table 1 the two large Pennsylvania districts are included in
the biennial column, but it was not possible to determine whether
districts belonging to other states in the third category should also
be there. Although most districts are in the biennial column, the
trend in recent years has been toward annual legislative sessions.

Not so typical of other urban school districts is that the school
board is appointed (by the judge of the Court of Common Pleas)
rather than elected.[12] As a result, the demands of the general public
in this district are probably less influential than in most others. It
is not clear, however, whether this produces larger budgets, smaller
budgets, or has any effect at all.[13]

While the local government has no major legal ties with the
model's school system, the state government does exercise control
over the budgetary process. For instance, it imposes an upper limit
on the real estate tax rate (as well as on all other taxes), which
may be increased only by special legislative act. In order to make
comparisons concerning this type of regulation, data compiled by
H. Thomas James, James A. Kelly, and Walter I. Garms have

[11] Appropriations from the state reimbursement could change slightly from
an odd to an even year if enrollment changed.

[12] NEA, *Local School Boards: Status and Practices* (Educational Research
Circular No. 6; Washington, D.C.: The Association, 1967); pp. 4, 14.

[13] H. Thomas James, James A. Kelly, and Walter I. Garms in *Determinants of Educational Expenditures in Large Cities of the United States*
(Stanford, Calif.: Stanford University, School of Education, 1966), pp.
117–118, have found no relationship between current spending and whether
a board is appointed or elected, but concede that the two values of the independent variable may each have positive effects in some locations and negative effects in others. Their results are based on data from 107 large districts
compiled in the years 1959–1960.

been used.[14] They define an "effective" state maximum property tax rate to exist where either the state sets a rate which cannot be legally exceeded or where the state's maximum can be exceeded but is not. The latter condition is included on the assumption that the regulations on surpassing the limit will be very restrictive. Table 1 shows that the model's district is in the minority with regard to the presence of an effective maximum rate. Although the state government plays a heavier role than usual in the revenue-formulation process, there is some evidence that it may not affect spending. James, Kelly, and Garms found no significant relation between current spending and a variable representing the presence or absence of an effective maximum rate.[15] And it should be remembered that the district's effective property tax rate was already found to be average, in spite of state control of the maximum rate.

Administrative Organization

An organization chart for the district appears in Figure 1.[16] At the top of the hierarchy are the board of education and the superintendent, who reports to the board. A step below is the department of business, headed by an associate superintendent. The next level consists of the educational operating divisions, each under the direction of an assistant superintendent. These divisions have authority over the operating personnel in the elementary and secondary schools and in some instances have staff sections reporting to them. Also on this level are a number of supplementary services and business functions, some of which are composed of various subunits. At the bottom of the hierarchy are several staff units, each headed by a director or a supervisor, who reports directly to the superintendent. They are responsible for providing educational

[14] *Ibid.*, pp. 144–145.
[15] *Ibid.*, pp. 121–123.
[16] As implied by the title of Figure 1, the organizational structure was being revised during this study.

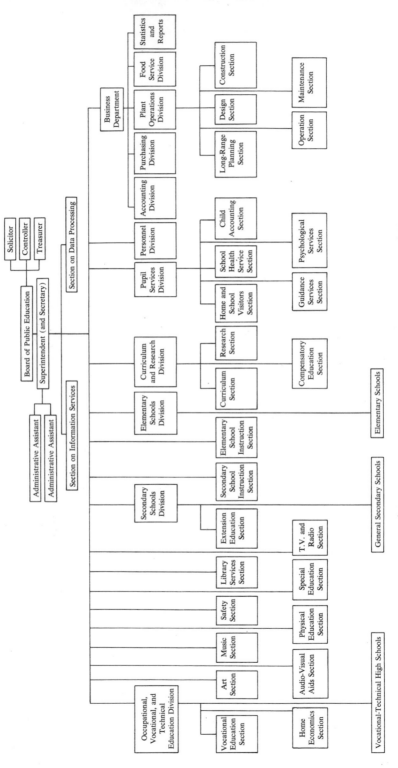

Figure 1. Interim Organizational Structure During Management Survey, September 1964

services in the areas of their specialty. Both an elementary (secondary) school division and an elementary (secondary) school instruction section are listed; the first is an operating unit, the other a staff unit.

Description of the Budget

The 1965 allocation provides an example of the composition of the operating budget. On the revenue side the real estate tax is the most significant item (52 percent of the total), while the state appropriation (23 percent) and the earned income tax (12 percent) are the next largest. The balance is made up primarily of other taxes and the carry-over from the preceding year.

Table 2—Comparison of the School District's Budget with the Model's Budget[a]

The District's Budget	
1. Salaries and benefits	$31,671,905
2. Other expenses	4,451,518
3. Capital outlay	1,330,104
4. Debt service	2,042,423
5. Tax refunds	400,000
6. Contingencies	100,000
	$39,995,950

The Model's Budget	
1. Fixed obligations	$33,563,765
2. Major-subunit materials	3,211,160
3. Major-subunit new personnel	643,983
4. Miscellaneous expenditures	2,227,042
5. New debt service	15,000
6. General salary increase	0
7. New fringe benefits	335,000
8. Special contingency	0
	$39,995,950

[a]The data are from the 1965 budget.

The expenditure side of the budget is divided into six broad categories including salaries and fringe benefits, other expenses, capital outlay, debt service, tax refunds, and contingencies. (See Table 2.) The main contents of the first category are self-explanatory. It also includes as a credit a provision for unexpended appropriations in the coming year, since budgeted spending usually exceeds actual spending for a variety of uncontrollable reasons, primarily teacher turnover. The second category consists of approved requests for supplies and for the repair and replacement (maintenance) of equipment. Supplies, which tend to be consumable items, are typically differentiated from equipment by having a unit cost less than some limit which varies from department to department. The second category also contains a number of miscellaneous items, of which the major ones are utility payments and pupil transportation. The capital-outlay section consists chiefly of approved requests for the purchase of new equipment as opposed to replacements. Debt service covers the principal and interest on bond issues, while the tax-refunds category is a provision for the return of tax payments in anticipation of court decisions on individual appeals. Finally, the contingency section includes a small amount for emergencies plus occasional provisions for special problems.

The Model's Budget

The budget developed for the model involves a rearrangement of the actual budget in order to highlight the decisions with which this study will be concerned. The realignment is shown in Table 2, where the six major categories of the school system are transformed into the model's eight. The first group, fixed obligations, consists of items more or less taken as given for decision-making purposes. The largest part is the salaries and benefits of personnel employed by the district at the start of budget preparation, minus any of these positions subsequently removed, and comes from Item 1 of the district's budget. The overwhelming share, the minuend, is fixed because it is set according to predetermined salary schedules. The subtrahend is subject to discretion and is considered as such in the model. The fixed-obligations category also includes debt service on bonds issued prior to budget preparation (from Item 4), the tax refunds of Item 5, and several miscellaneous appropriations from Items 1 and 2.

The second and third groups involve appropriations for what will be defined in Chapter 3 to be the "major" subunits of the administrative hierarchy. The materials group includes supplies and repairs and replacements from Item 2 and capital outlay from Item 3. New personnel, from Item 1, involves those additional positions allocated during budget preparation.

The fourth category is called miscellaneous spending. It consists of funds for the minor subunits including new personnel (from Item 1), supplies and repairs and replacements from Item 2, capital outlay from Item 3, and such miscellaneous accounts from Item 2 as utility payments and pupil transportation. It also contains the provision for unexpended appropriations from Item 1 and regular contingencies from Item 6.

The rest of the categories in the model's budget are debt service resulting from decisions made during budget preparation (from Item 4), a general salary increase and new fringe benefits as opposed to increases in existing ones from Item 1,[17] and a special-contingency provision from Item 6 for problems which might arise in the coming year.

In short, the rearrangement involves separating out in Item 1 of the model's budget decisions over which there exists little control and dealing with those over which discretion is exercised in the remaining items. Discretionary decisions of special interest are identified in Items 2, 3, 5, 6, 7, and 8, while the balance is lumped together into Item 4.

---

[17] It was not possible to separate increases in existing benefits for uncontrollable reasons (e.g., state regulations, increases in the number of employees) from increases arising out of the exercise of discretion. Therefore, they are all considered as part of fixed obligations.

Description of the Budgetary Process

The budget in the model's district covers the period from January to December. The first step in the process occurs when the state legislature convenes to enact laws, among them those affecting the budgets of local school districts. Since the legislature considers these matters only every odd-numbered year, this step enters the process only when the budget is being prepared for an even-numbered year.

The state's deliberations are important because they represent the only way in which the system's revenues can be sizeably increased. The legislature has the power to make changes in the formula by which state funds are allocated to the districts. It also controls the upper limit on the real estate tax rate and imposes various kinds of limits on the rates of all other levies. At the present time the school district is at the limit of all its tax rates; they may be increased only by special legislative acts.

The next step in preparing the budget occurs in the second quarter of the year. Forms are sent to the subunits in the administrative hierarchy so that they may enter their requests. Roughly speaking, there is a separate budget account number on these sheets for supplies, repairs and replacements, and capital outlay, along with the budget appropriation for the current year and the actual expenditures of the previous year. There is also an account number for each existing job in the section, but the corresponding wages are filled in by the accounting department because they are governed by a predetermined scale. Written justification must accompany requests for new personnel, supplies greater than the current appropriation, repairs and replacements, and capital outlay. Frequently, justifications for the last two items are provided only for amounts in excess of current appropriations.

Early in the third quarter the superintendent, business manager, and chief accountant (hereafter called the staff) make a preliminary review of budgetary requests. During their meetings, subunit heads may be called in to defend these requests. Their decisions result in a preliminary budget book which has the same format as the request forms, except that the request figures are replaced by the preliminarily approved outlays and a calculation is made for each account number of the difference between the appropriation for next year and this year.

Near the beginning of September the chief accountant starts to develop revenue forecasts for the coming year based on past revenue collections and an analysis of current economic conditions. The estimates are reviewed weekly and may be changed as new information becomes available. At the end of September a summary preliminary budget incorporating the revenue forecasts and the staff's preliminary spending decisions is prepared for presentation to the school board. Typically, no attempt is made at this point to equalize revenues and expenditures, but recommendations may be prepared to suggest how this could be accomplished.

In the beginning of October the school board, with the cooperation of the staff, begins its budget review. First, the revenue estimates are reviewed. The forecasts of the chief accountant are compared to those compiled by the city controller and by a private research organization. Expenditures are examined next in order to bring them into balance with revenues. The staff's decisions on department requests are reviewed. Then consideration is given to other major needs. The issue of a general salary increase is highlighted by a public meeting at which representatives of various employee groups present their requests. Debt service on a new bond issue is another major expenditure possibility.

When agreement between the staff and the board has been reached, a public hearing is held to present the budget. If necessary, changes are made after the presentation. Finally, the board meets to adopt the budget officially. This must be done by the Friday before the first Monday in December.

Outline of the Model

A flow chart of the model's version of the budgetary process appears in Chart 1. It is assumed that the budget for year $t+1$ is

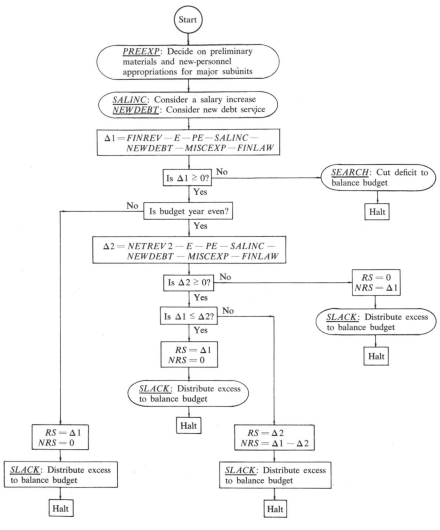

In this chart, the rounded boxes are for decisions which will be the major concern of this study. The underlined terms in these boxes identify the detailed flow charts which appear later.

Chart 1. Outline of the Model

compiled in year t. The revenue decisions of the state legislature and subunit requests are regarded as exogenous to the model.[18] The point of departure is a preliminary review made by the administrative staff of major-subunit requests ($PREEXP$), in which two preliminary allocations are made to each subunit. The first, for materials, is the sum of supplies, repairs and replacements, and capital outlay, since these items are not handled separately. The second, for new personnel, is a single amount for each subunit rather than a separate decision on each new position requested. The major-subunit allocations are also aggregated into the total preliminary materials appropriation (E) and the total preliminary new-personnel appropriation (PE). The other types of decisions made during the actual preliminary review are aggregated into a single prediction of preliminary miscellaneous appropriations ($MISCEXP$), which enters the model at a later point.

The next decisions are whether to grant a general salary increase ($SALINC$) and whether to issue any new bonds which would require an increase in the level of debt service ($NEWDEBT$) in the operating budget. Contrary to the actual situation, these choices are made in the model before forecasted revenues are compared to preliminary expenditures; the comparison is not a crucial factor in the determination of whether allocations will be made to these two areas in any given year. New debt service and a general salary increase were budgeted for 1954, for example, even though the revenue-expenditure comparison indicated a deficit was in the making. The factors which do influence the particular years in which these allocations will be made are discussed in Chapter 4.

The next step in the model is the calculation of the projected surplus or deficit for $t+1$ ($\Delta 1$), taking into consideration those decisions which have been made up to this point in the process. The revenue figure used in the calculation ($FINREV$) is taken from the district's final budget. Naturally, the revenue figure used by the

---

[18] No attempt will be made to analyze the manner in which the legislature's decisions are made. Subunit requests are studied separately in Chapter 7.

school system comes from the preliminary budget. The effect is that the model considers preliminary revenues and any subsequent revisions as given. The expenditure side of the calculation includes the spending decisions discussed above and the aforementioned prediction of preliminary miscellaneous appropriations (*MISCEXP*). It also includes what may be termed the preliminary value of fixed obligations (*FINLAW*).[19]

It is at this point that the school board becomes involved in budgeting decisions. If $\Delta 1$ is negative, certain appropriations are cut to balance the budget. This process (*SEARCH*) can affect the fixed-obligation, major materials, major new-personnel, and miscellaneous-spending categories. In addition, if decisions are being made to reduce appropriations, no new fringe benefits or special-contingency fund will be allocated.

If $\Delta 1 \geq 0$, the surplus must be distributed to balance the budget. This process (*SLACK*) can affect major materials and new personnel, fringe benefits, and the special-contingency fund. It requires a division of the available funds into recurring (*RS*) and nonrecurring (*NRS*) spending components. These components are determined using a prediction of the surplus or deficit for $t+2$ ($\Delta 2$), which in turn depends in part upon an exogenous factor, the district's forecast of revenues for $t+2$ minus net added spending to originate in that year (*NETREV* 2). The detailed aspects of the process will be discussed in Chapter 5.

The model involves a total of six key decisions, not all of which need be made every year. Two of these are decisions made by the staff alone: (1) preliminary appropriations of new personnel for the major subunits and (2) preliminary appropriations of materials

---

[19] At this point in the model *FINLAW* includes the salaries and benefits of positions existing at the start of budget preparation, debt service incurred prior to budget preparation, and the final budgeted values of such other accounts as tax refunds; all are considered exogenous. The remaining component, any elimination of positions, takes place only during the school board review. It is predicted later in the model and subtracted from the preliminary value of *FINLAW*.

for the major subunits. The rest are decisions made jointly by the staff and the board: (3) a general salary increase; (4) debt service on a new bond issue; (5) a process to balance the budget when preliminary expenditures (the sum of the expenditures used in the calculation of Δ 1) exceed forecasted revenues; and (6) a distribution of excess funds to balance the budget when forecasted revenues exceed preliminary expenditures.

The next three chapters will explain the manner in which these six decisions are made. A detailed account of the sources of the data used in analyzing the decisions is found in Appendix I.

The Model and the Model's Budget

It is now possible to reexamine Table 2 in order to see how the model's budget is compiled. The overwhelming share of fixed obligations (Item 1) is considered given, except that an allowance is made for the prediction of the elimination of employee positions which may occur when a deficit is to be removed. The major-subunit materials and new-personnel allocations (Items 2 and 3) are the results of a set of preliminary decisions and possibly the use of certain steps in a budget-balancing procedure. Miscellaneous spending (Item 4) arises from an aggregate prediction and is not considered a key decision; it may be affected by the need to eliminate a deficit. Nothing need be pointed out at this time about new debt service (Item 5) and a general salary increase (Item 6), except that they are handled in the model. New fringe benefits (Item 7) and the special contingency (Item 8) occur only when a distribution of excess funds is made.

3

Preliminary Subunit

Allocations

The initial step in the detailed analysis of the model involves the process by which materials and new personnel are preliminarily allocated to the major subunits. This process is labeled *PREEXP* in Chart 1. Before analysis begins it is important to mention that in many years it is not necessary for budget-balancing procedures to be used to revise these particular preliminary decisions. Accordingly, the conclusions of this chapter will frequently provide the complete picture on the final materials and new-personnel allocations.

The Major Subunits

The budgetary requests of the subunits found in Figure 1 fall into three categories: salaries and benefits (Item 1 of the district's budget), other expenses (Item 2), and capital outlay (Item 3). Each of these three is essentially subdivided into general control (mainly business functions), auxiliary services (guidance and other pupil services), and instruction (educational services). Some of the units at the divisional level and above may make requests which fit into any or all of the three subdivisions and therefore cannot be associated with a particular one. The staff units below the divisional level, however, usually keep all their requests within one subdivision.

Because of problems encountered in collecting data (which are discussed in Appendix I), the largest components of just instructional appropriations were individually analyzed. Of the staff units which belong in the instructional area, only those with materials appropriations greater than $10,000 in the 1965 budget were selected as major subunits. A list appears in Table 3. For the pur-

Table 3—The Major Subunits

Art
Audio-visual aids
Elementary education instruction section
Elementary education
Kindergarten
Home economics
Library services
Music
Physical education
"Schools"
Secondary schools instruction section
Business education
English
Foreign languages
Science
Social studies
Special education
Television education
Vocational education

pose of analyzing materials, the elementary-instruction section was divided into two components and the secondary-instruction section into five, since requests came from these seven sources. In analyzing new personnel the two staff units were used instead, since requests emanated from them.

The new-personnel requests of the staff subunits are usually for educational supervisors and office staff. The materials requests are for items in the particular specialty of the subunit.

As it turns out, the largest appropriations in the instructional area are earmarked for the schools in general rather than for a particular educational specialty. These accounts, requested for the most part by the department of business and various divisions, appear under a "Schools" heading in the budget. Therefore, "Schools" is considered to be the final major subunit.

Because of the large appropriations (generally over $100,000) in each of the pertinent accounts of the "Schools" subunit, they are treated individually in the model. (See Table 4.) Repairs and

Table 4—The "Schools" Subunit

New personnel	Requested by
Committee work	Division of Curriculum and Research
Counselors	Division of Pupil Services
Department chairmen	Secondary School Instruction Section
Principals	Divisions of Elementary and Secondary Schools
School clerks	Divisions of Elementary Schools, Secondary Schools, and Pupil Services
Teachers	Divisions of Elementary and Secondary Schools

Materials	Requested by
Administration building repairs and alterations	Department of Business
Principals' office supplies	Divisions of Elementary and Secondary Schools
School building repairs and alterations	Department of Business
School equipment repairs and capital outlay	Department of Business
School furniture repairs and capital outlay	Division of Purchasing
School room supplies	Divisions of Elementary and Secondary Schools
Textbooks	Divisions of Elementary and Secondary Schools

replacements and capital outlay for the same item (such as school furniture) are combined, even though treated separately in the budget, because there is no clear-cut difference between them. The new-personnel accounts were selected by taking only those for which at least one request over $10,000 had been made from 1961 to 1965. Although not an appropriation for new personnel, committee work, a provision for the summer employment of principals and teachers to work on curriculum revision, is included here because it involves salaries and was in excess of $10,000 in the 1965 budget. The supply, repair and replacement, and capital-outlay accounts were those over $10,000 in the 1965 budget.

Routine Materials Decisions

The rules followed by the staff when they make preliminary materials allocations to the major subunits were studied by considering routine decisions first and then more complicated ones. An important finding of the interviews with staff members was that if a materials request is close to the level of current appropriations it is usually routinely approved; otherwise, it is intensively reviewed and more likely to be cut. For the purpose of developing a useful decision rule from this information, two matters must be clarified. It is necessary, first of all, to recall that a subunit may have different preliminary and final appropriations owing to intervening budget-balancing procedures. In this situation the appropriate current appropriation level against which to compare requests must be found. It appears that the preliminary allocation is usually used, since any amount added or subtracted during the school board review is generally considered nonrecurring. For example, in the 1960 budget a distribution of excess funds for materials was made, but in the 1961 preliminary budget, appropriation cuts were made back to preliminary 1960 levels. Also, in the 1963 budget materials appropriations were reduced during the board's review, but in the 1964 budget no major subunit received less than its 1963 preliminary allocation unless it requested less.

Second, it is necessary to decide on the range within which requests are usually approved, since the staff was not precise in specifying its limits. In Table 5 data are presented for the five budgets from 1961 to 1965 ($t+1$ runs from 1961 to 1965). During those years all requests equal to current preliminary appropriations were approved. When requests were less than or greater than current preliminary appropriations, they were cut. This tendency exists

Table 5—The Number of Approved Requests

	Number of requests for $t+1 <$ Preliminary allocation in t	Number of requests for $t+1 =$ Preliminary allocation in t	Number of requests for $t+1 >$ Preliminary allocation in t	Total
Number of approved requests	7	26	41	74
Number of cut requests	3	0	36	39
Number of increased requests[a]	0	0	2	2
Total	10	26	79	115

[a]It was possible to find the rationale for only one of these occurrences. It involved the allowance of a relatively small increase in the operating budget of a subunit in lieu of a relatively large decrease in the money normally appropriated from the bond fund for this unit.

even when the two magnitudes are quite near each other. It seems, therefore, that the point at which the two are equal is the only clear-cut range within which to include routine decisions.

One final qualification is necessary in order to state a decision rule. Even though it appears that requests less than current preliminary appropriations are nonroutine in nature, serious errors do not arise in the model by including them in the routine category. Only 3 out of the 115 requests in Table 5 are less than their current appropriations and also cut.

It is now possible to state an operational definition of a routine decision incorporating all this information: *A routine decision is made on a request for* t+1 *which is less than or equal to the corresponding preliminary appropriation in* t.

In the model, the decision rule which applies to routine decisions is:

Rule 1: Approve all routine requests.

Nonroutine Materials Decisions and Revenue Expectations

During the staff's meetings, large materials requests relative to current preliminary appropriations act as a signal for intensive review. This may mean examining letters of justification or asking department heads to defend their requests.

Two important factors influence these nonroutine decisions. The first is the staff's expectations of how much additional funds will be available the next year. As has been pointed out, such expectations are based on general impressions; revenue forecasts are not begun until later in the process. The purpose of this section is to develop an operational measure of these general impressions for any particular year.

The key to this problem is the realization that the staff's impressions should be influenced only by expectations of large changes in the availability of funds. Consequently, it is necessary to determine how large changes may occur. On the revenue side the legislature's decisions with regard to tax rates, the parameters of the state appropriation formula, and new sources of revenues may all cause fluctuations in the funds available to the school district. If the budget year is odd, then the legislature met in $t-1$ and its decisions are known during the initial review in t. If the budget year is even, then the legislature meets in t and its decisions may or may not be known when the initial review is made. If the budget year is even and the state house of representatives has passed a bill affecting the district's revenues before the initial review begins, then the staff members, when they meet, will expect the bill to become a law. A bill that has not passed the house prior to the initial review will not be expected to affect the district's revenues.

The effect of local economic conditions on tax bases may also produce a significant change in the coming year's revenues. The earned income tax, the mercantile levy based on wholesale and retail sales, and the personal property tax based on stocks, bonds, and other evidences of indebtedness are the most likely items to be affected. Since expectations with regard to the influence of economic conditions are intuitive at this point, a method of measur-

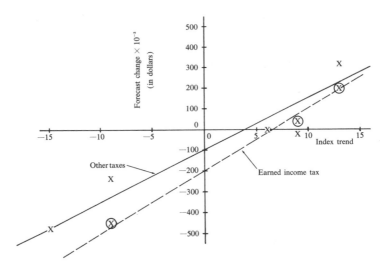

Figure 2. Effect of Local Economic Conditions on Expectations

ing their impact had to be developed. The first step was to use a monthly, seasonally adjusted index of general business activity for the metropolitan area.[1] Business activity in that part of the year prior to the staff's meetings was estimated by calculating the trend in the index from January to June. Specifically, the averages of the May and June values and the January and February values were calculated. Then the latter was subtracted from the former.

Next, it was assumed that the forecasts of the three tax bases in the preliminary budget approximate, at least up to a normal random error with mean zero, the intuitive notions of the staff during the initial review.[2] As a result, the changes in the tax base forecasts

[1] The index appears in "Tables," *Pittsburgh Business Review,* 32, no. 6 (March, 1962)–34, no. 9 (October, 1964). Prior to March 1962 a different set of base years had been used. The values from January 1960 to February 1962, in terms of the current base, were obtained from Robert Pratt, editor.

[2] On the basis of this assumption it might be argued that the preliminary budget forecasts for $t+1$ can be used to approximate the staff's impressions during the initial review for that year. On the other hand, since the preliminary forecasts occur after the staff's review, the predictive ability of the model would be forfeited in this area.

from the preliminary budget for t to that for $t+1$ represent the changes in the staff's notions from the initial review in $t-1$ to that in t. Then it was possible to plot, using past data, the forecast changes from the preliminary budget for t to that for $t+1$ versus the index trend in t. This is done in Figure 2, using data from the 1961 to 1965 budgets. Here, the dependent variable is measured in units of dollars rather than in the units of the tax base, since no changes in tax rates occurred over the five-year period. The earned income tax is plotted separately because it went into effect more recently than the others and there is less data for it. In both cases, a line was fitted through the points by eye because of the paucity of data. Given the value of the index trend in any year, the lines can be used to approximate the staff's impressions of the effect of local economic conditions on the following year's revenues.

It is interesting to observe that these lines have negative intercepts. It takes, for example, a trend of about $+6\frac{1}{2}$ points to project an increase for the earned income tax—a noteworthy amount when one considers that the largest absolute value of the trend in any of the five years studied was 15 points. These findings are supported by the opinion of one staff member who felt that revenues tended to be underestimated in order to protect against the situation in which actual revenues turned out to be less than anticipated and spending consequently had to be cut.

A final possible source of added revenues involves the estimated carry-over of funds from t to $t+1$; that is, an estimate of the difference between actual revenues and expenditures in t. Ordinarily, not much is expected from this source. In considering the seven normal instances from the 1958 to 1965 budgets, the estimate was found to be over $275,000 only once, while twice it was zero. Thus, only in an exceptional case is the carry-over assumed by the model to influence general impressions. Exceptions occur because the estimate of actual revenues for t includes the actual carry-over from $t-1$. Since the latter quantity is known when the preliminary staff meetings are held, a large amount can influence general impressions for $t+1$.

It is also possible to discover how large, uncontrollable changes in expenditures may occur in the coming year. According to the theories developed in Chapter 4, a general salary increase fits into this category. It is usually estimated to be about $1,000,000, but under certain conditions spelled out in that chapter, the amount can be more. The only other significant, uncontrollable expenditure is the automatic, yearly salary increase which occurs as employees move to the next step in their salary schedules.

Now that the significant revenue and expenditure changes have been described, it is necessary to discuss how they are combined into what shall be called the General Impressions Measure (G.I.M.). First, the values of all changes are added for any particular year. If the sum is greater than 0, a G.I.M. value of "high" is assigned to the year; if the sum is less than or equal to 0, a "low" is assigned. Because some theories concerning the effects of expectations on preliminary materials decisions will be tested later, it is necessary to classify the five years for which there is data (1961 to 1965) as either high or low. It was determined that 1962, 1964, and 1965 were high years, while 1961 and 1963 were found to be low years. (See Appendix II for calculations.)

Priority Effects on Nonroutine Materials Decisions

Previously, it was mentioned that there are two factors which influence preliminary nonroutine materials decisions for the major subunits. The first is the expectations of added funds. The second, to be discussed now, is the ranking of materials accounts in an informal priority system. The existence of priority levels was inferred from interviews with the staff.

The most-favored group (the first priority level) is composed of major-subunit materials requested by the members of the "cabinet," an informally organized body which meets weekly at the request of the superintendent to discuss educational policy. It consists of the superintendent, the associate superintendent for business, and the six assistant superintendents. They are in charge of elementary education, secondary education, pupil services, curricu-

Table 6—Priority Classification of the Major Materials Accounts

First priority level	Second priority level	Third priority level
Administration building repairs and alterations	Audio-visual aids	Art
Principals' office supplies	Elementary education	Business education
School building repairs and alterations	English	Home economics
School equipment repairs and capital outlay	Foreign languages	Music
School room supplies	Kindergarten	Physical education
Textbooks	Library services	Vocational education (prior to 1964)
Vocational education (1964 and after)	School furniture	
	Science	
	Social studies	
	Special education	
	Television education	

lum and research, personnel, and occupational, vocational, and technical (O.V.T.) education. The major-subunit materials requested by cabinet members are listed in Table 6 under the heading of "First priority level." All of them, with the exception of vocational education, belong to the "Schools" subunit.

The most recent addition to the cabinet (the first priority) is the new O.V.T. division. Its appropriations make up the budget of the old vocational-education staff section. Hence, although two separate units actually exist, for our purposes they may be considered identical. The exact date that vocational education achieved cabinet status could not be pinned down. The starting date was assumed to be in June 1963, when the school board accepted the study which led to the redesign of the program.[3] As a result, in Table 6 vocational education appears in the first priority only for the 1964 budget and after.

The second most-favored group (the second priority level) consists of major materials which the school system considers to be academic in nature. The academic subject areas—elementary edu-

[3] See Donald D. Dauwalder, *Vocational Education in the Pittsburgh Public Schools* (Pittsburgh, Pa.: The Pittsburgh Board of Public Education, 1963).

cation, science, English, social studies, and foreign languages—are included here. In addition, kindergarten and special education belong in this level because they are areas in which academic subject matter is taught to particular groups of students. The second priority also contains instructional services used primarily for academic teaching: audio-visual aids, television education, and school libraries. Finally, since most school furniture is appropriated for the academic areas, that account is included here.

The least-favored group (the third priority level) includes the nonacademic subject areas of the curriculum: art, physical education, music, home economics, business education, and vocational education (prior to the 1964 budget).

It should be noted that the priority concept is not a completely static theory. One dynamic mechanism which takes into consideration that in the long run accounts change their priorities as the goals of the organization shift exists. This mechanism is the ability of second and third priority accounts to move to the top level by achieving cabinet status. Vocational education is the latest example of such a shift. The recent history of its appropriations is presented

Table 7—Vocational Education Appropriations

Budget year $(t+1)$	1961	1962	1963	1964	1965
Ratio of the preliminary appropriation in $t+1$ to the preliminary appropriation in t	1.00	1.03	1.02	1.46	2.32

in Table 7. It is obvious that a radical shift occurred starting with the 1964 budget. This change in budgeting policy was accompanied by a shift to cabinet status and may be viewed as an attempt by the superintendent to achieve status congruence for this unit with respect to other sections.[4] Status congruence exists between two

[4] See George Caspar Homans, *Social Behavior: Its Elementary Forms* (New York: Harcourt, Brace and World, 1961), Chap. 12, for a thorough treatment of status congruence.

subunits when the factors which differentiate them are all greater for one than for the other. Thus, it would be incongruent for vocational education to receive appropriations as if it were in the first priority, but still remain in the third priority. The establishment of congruence, at least along the dimensions of appropriations and priority, serves the purpose of making it clear to all concerned that a shift in status has occurred. This reduction in ambiguity tends to produce swifter changes in behavior towards the subunit on the part of the rest of the organization and the community at large than if much ambiguity remained.

Selection of Decision Rules

These theories concerning the expectations and priority effects can be useful as guides in the determination of rules for nonroutine materials decisions. Any nonroutine request may be classified according to its priority level and whether it is made for a high or low-expectations year. The result is the 3×2 table of classification depicted in Table 8. A decision rule may now be associated with each of the six cells where cell ij is the one in the ith row $(i = 1, 2, 3)$ and j^{th} column $(j = 1, 2)$.

Table 8—Table of Classification for Nonroutine Decisions

	High expectations	Low expectations
First priority level		
Second priority level		
Third priority level		

In order to find appropriate rules the seventy-nine nonroutine decisions of the 1961 to 1965 budgets were classified according to the cells to which they belonged. In examining decisions for cells 11, 12, and 21, it was apparent that most of their requests were approved; this could not be said of the other cells. The contingency table in Table 9 summarizes the pertinent information and can be used to test whether the probability of approving a request is greater for cells 11, 12, and 21 than for the rest. The null hypothesis of no difference in probabilities was rejected at the 0.005 signifi-

Table 9—Justification for Rule 2

	Number of approved requests	Number of cut requests[a]	Total
Cells 11, 12, 21	33	9	42
Other cells	8	29	37
Total	41	38	79

[a]The first two numbers in this column each contain a request which was increased *above* what was asked for.

cance level, using the test for independence. The following decision rule is the result:

> *Rule 2:* If the G.I.M. is high, then approve the nonroutine request of any account in the first or second priority. If the G.I.M. is low, then approve the nonroutine request of any account in the first priority.

The nonroutine decisions for the remaining cells are predicted by multiplying a parameter associated with each cell by the current preliminary appropriation of each account in the cell. But, if the result is greater than the request, then the prediction is set equal to that request, since out of the 115 decisions investigated over the five-year period only 2 involved more than what was asked.[5] As an example the rule used for cell 31 is:

> *Rule 3:* If the G.I.M. is high, then to determine the preliminary appropriation for an account in the third priority, mul-

[5] When tests were conducted, the model used this provision in only 2 instances out of a possible 35.

tiply a parameter times the current preliminary appropriation. If the parameter times the current preliminary appropriation is greater than the request, then allocate funds equal in magnitude to the latter.

The same rule applies when the G.I.M. is low to the second and third priorities except that different parameters are used in each case.

The three parameters were estimated using the following procedure: For each nonroutine request in the 1961 to 1965 budgets that fit into one of the three cells, the preliminary appropriation in $t+1$ divided by the preliminary appropriation in t was calculated. The parameter associated with each cell was chosen to be the median of the ratios in each cell. The median was used so that a few relatively large ratios due chiefly to extraneous circumstances would not have a great effect on the estimates. The estimated values were 1.12 for cell 31, 1.08 for cell 22, and 1.00 for cell 32. Further information concerning the samples in each cell is provided in Appendix III.

Analysis of the Expectations and Priority Effects

One way of exploring the influence of expectations and priorities is to study approved versus cut nonroutine requests in the 1961 to 1965 budgets. In Table 10 the number of such approvals $(B = R)$ and reductions $(B < R)$ are classified into the six priority-expectations combinations.

An examination of the table bears out the theories discussed earlier. Whether expectations are high or low, the fraction of requests approved is greatest for the first priority and next greatest for the second priority; that is, the priority effect asserts itself in high and low years. In addition, whether we examine the first, second, or third priority, a greater fraction of requests are granted in high as opposed to low years; in other words, the expectations effect exists for all three groups.

Statistical support for the existence of a priority effect may be

Table 10—The Number of Approved Requests

	High expectations			Low expectations		
	$B = R$[a]	$B < R$	Fraction of requests approved	$B = R$	$B < R$	Fraction of requests approved
First priority level	11	0	1.00	8	2	0.80
Second priority level	15	6	0.71	5	13	0.28
Third priority level	4	6	0.40	0	9	0.00

[a]The first and third numbers in this column each include a request for which $B > R$.

provided by testing whether the probability of approving a request depends upon its priority classification. This involves constructing a 3×2 contingency table from the data of Table 10. The rows stand for the three priority classifications, while the columns represent $B = R$ and $B < R$. A test of independence rejected the null hypothesis of no difference in probabilities at less than the .005 level.

Whether the probability of approving a request is greater in high as opposed to low-expectations years may be tested in a similar manner. In order to provide the evidence a 2×2 contingency table whose rows are for high and low expectations and whose columns are the same as in the previous table must be formed. A test of independence rejected the null hypothesis of no difference in probabilities at the .005 level.

Another type of analysis was conducted by studying changes in nonroutine appropriations over the five-year period for which there was data. For each nonroutine decision the preliminary appropriation in $t+1$ divided by the preliminary appropriation in t was determined. Then the seventy-five ratios with non-zero denominators were classified into the six cells of Table 8. Detailed information on the characteristics of the samples is provided in Appendix III.

In conducting statistical tests of the expectations and priority effects, various groups of observations drawn from the cells of Table 8 were compared for differences in location. Since nonparametric tests were employed, it was not necessary to specify any particular measure of location such as the mean or median. The independence assumption may be strained, however, since ratios for the same account in different years are able to appear in the same group.

The expectations effect was tested by comparing the locations of the sample formed by merging cells 11, 21, and 31 (high expectations) with the sample resulting from the combination of cells 12, 22, and 32 (low expectations). Using the rank-sum test, the hypothesis of no difference was rejected at a significance level less than 0.02.[6] And the direction of the test statistic indicated that the location of the first sample was higher than that of the second.

In examining the priority effect, the location of the sample formed from cells 11 and 12 (first priority) was compared to that of the sample composed of cells 21 and 22 (second priority), and then the latter location was compared to that of the sample from cells 31 and 32 (third priority). The first of these tests was not significant at the 0.05 level, but the second was at a level less than 0.03, and the statistic was in the desired direction. Apparently, when the observations from high and low years are merged there is no reason to distinguish between the first and second priorities.

Next the relationships among particular pairs of cells, especially adjoining ones, were examined to see if any further insights could be obtained. A significant difference, for example, might exist between the first two priorities when expectations had a given value.

---

[6] Wilfrid J. Dixon and Frank J. Massey, *Introduction to Statistical Analysis,* 2d ed. (New York: McGraw-Hill, 1957), p. 289.

Table 11—Values of the Statistic for the Multiple-Comparison Test

	High expectations	Low expectations
First priority level	42.5	46.9
Second priority level	47.4	32.8
Third priority level	37.7	12.3

In order to make several pairwise comparisons, it was necessary to use a nonparametric multiple-comparison test.[7] The test indicated that the only significant differences in location at the 0.05 level involved cells 12 and 32, and 21 and 32. Although the number of significant pairs was very low, the results are nevertheless useful. They show that the primary reason for the pattern of confirmation and rejection noted in the three tests mentioned above is due to the relatively low values in cell 32. More important, it appears that the relationship between the expectations and priority effects is not a simple additive one; rather, these two variables interact in their effect on changes in appropriations.

The presence of an interaction effect is more conspicuously revealed in Table 11, where the values of the statistic used in the multiple-comparison test are recorded. These numbers measure the locations of the samples in each cell relative to each other.[8] Suppose those values of 40 or over are classified as high locations, those from 30 to 39 as medium, and those below 30 as low. The following tendencies, except for a minor discrepancy in cell 11's value, will be observed: (1) the first priority is unaffected by expectations; (2) the second priority falls relative to the first and the third falls relative to the second in lean years; and (3) the second

[7] See Rupert G. Miller, *Simultaneous Statistical Inference* (New York: McGraw-Hill, 1966), pp. 165–172, for a description of the test.
[8] The values were computed by arranging the 75 observations in numerical order and ranking them so that 1 was assigned to the lowest and 75 to the highest. Then the ranks of the observations in each cell were added and the sum divided by the number of observations in each cell.

priority rises to the level of the first and the third rises almost to the level of the first in good years. In other words, the priority effect is blurred when expectations are high and pronounced when they are low.

It must be reiterated that this tendency in the data is not statistically significant. It does deserve mention, however, both because it is an eminently plausible strategy for the administration to follow and also because it conforms to theories developed elsewhere.[9]

It appears, therefore, that when financial resources are expected to be abundant the staff tends to go along with subunit aspirations as reflected in their requests. Under adverse expectations, however, the staff is forced to choose among the subunits; the priority system is the result.

Preliminary Decisions on New Personnel

The major subunits do not request their entire personnel budgets over again each year. The salaries of employees working for the school system at the start of budget preparation are considered given during the preliminary review and are filled in by the accounting department according to predetermined schedules. Since it was not possible to find a situation in which a request for a decrease in the number of employees was made, we may assume that only requests for more personnel are considered by the staff. Apparently, appropriations for existing employees represent a base which is not reviewed; concentration is reserved for the question of increases

[9] For example, the "organizational slack" phenomenon discussed by Richard M. Cyert and James G. March in *A Behavioral Theory of the Firm* (Englewood Cliffs, N.J.: Prentice-Hall, 1963), pp. 36–38. In their view, slack consists of payments to subunits in excess of the amounts needed to maintain them in the organization. During boom periods firms acquire excess resources and distribute them, but during downturns cuts are made in these payments in order to insure organizational survival. My own observations elaborate on this theory by suggesting that slack is neither distributed nor eliminated in an egalitarian manner.

over the base. This result is similar to that for preliminary materials decisions; the essential difference is that here the process has become a bit more institutionalized.

Three major factors influence decisions on new personnel. Two of these, the expectations of added revenues in the coming year and the informal priority system, have already been introduced. The

Table 12—Priority Classification of the Major Personnel Accounts

First priority level	Second priority level	Third priority level
Committee work	Audio-visual aids	Art
Counselors	Elementary instruction	Home economics
Principals	Library services	Music
School clerks	Secondary instruction	Physical education
Teachers	and department	Vocational education
Vocational education	chairmen	(prior to 1964)
(1964 and after)	Special education	
	Television education	

new-personnel accounts in each of the three priority levels were selected using the same criteria employed for materials; they are listed in Table 12. In addition to these two, new employees also are considered recurring obligations which, in contrast to increases in materials appropriations, are not easily eliminated once budgeted. Clearly, the reasons for such a policy are due to its effect on recruiting, turnover, and employee morale. As a result, a cautious attitude exists in approving new-personnel requests, especially in lean years. For example, during the late 1950's, a fiscally tight period, the school board put a freeze on additional employees.

In order to analyze the effects of these three variables, data from the 1961 to 1965 budgets were utilized. Since there were not very many requests for new personnel during this period, the data were aggregated rather than examined on an individual-account basis, so that any trends might be more easily revealed. Table 13

Table 13—New-Personnel Data

	High-expectations years			Low-expectations years		
	Request total (R)	Preliminary budget total (B)	B/R	Request total (R)	Preliminary budget total (B)	B/R
First priority level	$566,265	$561,685	0.99	$ 56,600	$0	0.00
Second priority level[a]	440,696 *36,516*	68,008 *19,428*	0.15 *0.53*	290,500 *12,000*	0 *0*	0.00 *0.00*
Third priority level	53,600	20,480	0.38	0	0	—

[a]Italicized numbers exclude special education.

presents the total amount requested by and appropriated to the accounts in each priority for low and high-expectation years. The data for the second priority are given with and without special education. This subunit consistently makes very large requests, very little of which are ever preliminarily approved. For reasons to be discussed shortly, committee work was treated separately.

The criterion selected for evaluation purposes is the proportion of requests which is allocated in the budget (B/R). It is not feasible to look at the ratio of preliminary appropriations in $t+1$ to preliminary appropriations in t as was done for materials, because preliminary allocations to some accounts in the first priority (especially teachers) are so large that a percentage increase in them, comparable to that of most other accounts, could not typically be afforded.

The expectations effect does seem to exist, since the top two groups receive a larger proportion of their requests in abundant years. This cannot be determined for the third priority. The priority effect also is observable; when expectations are high, the first group does better than the second, which in turn fares better than the third (provided special education is eliminated). Furthermore, when expectations are low, the first group is not given less consideration than the second. Whether the second fares at least as well as the third cannot be determined. The relative caution in dealing with personnel requests as compared to materials can be observed by noticing that in lean periods none are approved, while in high years only the top priority tends to get all of its requests approved.

On the basis of what was learned about preliminary new-personnel decisions the following decision rule was formulated for the model:

> *Rule 4:* If the G.I.M. is high, approve all personnel requests from the first priority. If it is low, do not approve any personnel requests from this group. Do not approve any personnel requests from the other priorities whether the G.I.M. is high or low.

The rule is rather naive and suggests that this is an area deserving of a more intensive examination. On the other hand, it does reflect the ideas presented above concerning expectations, priorities, and cautiousness, albeit in a crude manner. New-personnel decisions do not involve a large sector of the budget—especially when the G.I.M. is low. Therefore, it is not expected that the rule will lead to large errors in the model.

Committee work, which is requested by a cabinet member, provides summer pay for those engaged in curriculum revision. The district's policy of including it with the salary accounts was followed in order to facilitate the comparison of predictions to actual appropriations. Since its entire budget must be requested over again each year, however, the staff treats it as a top-priority materials account. Consequently, the appropriate rule is to approve the entire request whether the G.I.M. is high or low.

Preliminary Decisions on Miscellaneous Expenditures

Miscellaneous spending contains the provision for unexpended appropriations, new personnel for the minor subunits, materials for

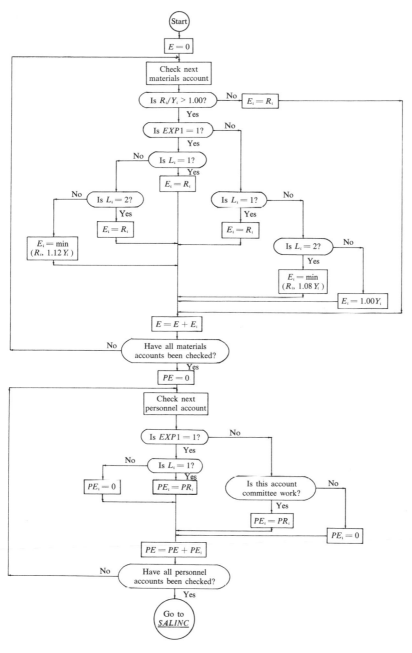

Chart 2. *PREEXP*

the minor subunits, regular contingencies, and several miscellaneous accounts. The unexpended appropriations portion is predicted by using its current final budget value. New personnel is assumed to be zero since it actually turns out to be an insignificant sum. The balance is predicted by multiplying a parameter, whose value depends upon whether the G.I.M. is high or low, by the total current preliminary allocation for these accounts. The parameter was estimated in the following manner: For each of the budgets from 1961 to 1965 the ratio of the preliminary allocation for these accounts in $t+1$ to the preliminary allocation in t was determined. Then the three ratios for the high years were averaged, as were the two ratios for the low years. If the G.I.M. is high, then the parameter is set equal to the first average (1.07); if the G.I.M. is low, it takes on the value of the second (0.98).

Explanation of Chart 2

The flow diagram of preliminary decisions on major subunit materials and new personnel appears in Chart 2. Initially, the total preliminary materials allocation to the major subunits (E) is zero. The decision process begins with the examination of materials requests on an individual basis. If the request of the ith account (R_i) is not greater than the current preliminary appropriation (Y_i), it is considered routine and the model's prediction (E_i) is to approve it.

If the request is nonroutine, an inquiry is made to see if expectations for the coming year and, consequently, the value of the G.I.M. are high $(EXP\ 1 = 1)$. If this is true, then the priority level of the ith account (L_i) must be determined. If the account is in the first level $(L_i = 1)$, the model's prediction is to approve the request. If the account is in the second level $(L_i = 2)$, the request is also approved. If the account is in the third level $(L_i = 3)$, the model's prediction is the smaller of the request or 1.12 times the current preliminary appropriation.

If expectations for the coming year (the value of the G.I.M.) are low $(EXP\ 1 = 0)$, a similar process is followed. If the ith

account is in the top level, its request is approved. If it is in the second level, the prediction is either the request or 1.08 times the current preliminary appropriation. If the account is in the third level, then its prediction is 1.00 times the current preliminary appropriation.

After all materials decisions have been made and the value of E calculated, the model moves on to examine personnel requests individually. Initially, the total preliminary new-personnel allocation to the major subunits (PE) is zero. If expectations are high, then the priority level of the ith account must be determined. If the account is in the first level, the model's prediction (PE_i) is to approve the request (PR_i). Otherwise, it receives no new personnel. If expectations are low and the account in question is committee work, its request is approved. Otherwise, its request is denied. Once all personnel accounts have been examined and the value of PE determined, the model moves on to consider a general salary increase (the $SALINC$ process).

4
Major Long-Run
Commitments

A general salary increase (*SALINC*) and new debt service (*NEW-DEBT*) are the next set of decisions made by the model. Each decision involves two components: a timing aspect, which dictates the particular years in which the budget will be affected, and an amount aspect, which controls how much will be allocated in those years.

General Salary Increases

In the Marshallian theory of wage determination the firm's wage rate and the marginal revenue product of labor tend toward equality. This viewpoint has been questioned for many years by those with a process-oriented approach to the problem. When it is applied to wage determination in the public sector, the theory is clearly even less appropriate as a descriptive framework, since one component of the marginal revenue product, the product price, is typically absent, while the other component, the marginal physical product of labor, cannot be readily measured. In addition, and perhaps because of these two qualifications, institutional factors and political influences seem to play more fundamental roles in the public sector than they do in the private.

Owing to the complexity of the problem, it is little wonder that no adequate theory of salary determination has yet been developed for the public sector. In the field of education, for example, it has usually been possible only to list such variables as salaries paid by other districts, the cost of living, teaching load, and ability to pay which undoubtedly influence salary increases.[1] For the most part, the construction of testable hypotheses which explain the precise manner in which these types of factors affect compensation decisions has been neglected.[2] In the following discussion it will be explained how the model's school district solves the difficult problem of salary determination—a finding which should contribute to the development of the needed salary-determination theory.

The district's occupational groups consist of teachers, other professionals, such as principals and counselors, and nonprofessionals, such as clerks and custodians. An attempt to compile a complete salary-increase history from the 1954 to 1965 budgets for every occupation was made, but it proved to be an impossible task—especially for the minor ones. Fortunately, this problem did not exist for the category of teachers, who represent about two-thirds of all employees.

Interviews and analysis of the data revealed that there is a strong tendency for all employees to receive increases at the same time. In the 1954 to 1965 budgets six of these general salary increases were granted, insofar as can be told, to all personnel; any probable exceptions were in the nonprofessional class. There were only a few occasions when particular groups received increases by themselves. Nonprofessionals with industrial counterparts have enjoyed raises in order to keep pace with wage levels in the local labor market. There were also two cases in which groups without counterparts obtained raises, but these resulted from salary-schedule reclassifications. Since these exceptional occasions involved rela-

---

[1] See, for example, William Everett Rosenstengel and Jefferson N. Eastmond, *School Finance* (New York: Ronald Press, 1957), p. 338.

[2] A notable exception is Charles S. Benson, *The Economics of Public Education* (Boston: Houghton Mifflin, 1961), pp. 415–423, whose theories focus on a salary-comparison process as the crucial factor.

Table 14—General Salary Increases

Budget	Increase granted	Source	Employees	Amount	ΔT[a]	CD[b]
1954	Yes	District	All	$ 492,000	$200	0
1955	No					2
1956	Yes	District	All	1,873,000	400	0
1957	Yes	{State / District	{Teachers / Others	{?[c] / ?[c]	{400[d] / —	{9
1958	No					7
1959	No					1
1960	Yes	District	All	1,207,000	300	0
1961	No					4
1962	Yes	District	All	1,697,000	700	0
1963	No					13
1964	Yes	{State / District	{Teachers / Others	{282,000 / 233,000	{0[e] / —	{8
1965	No					4

[a]ΔT = increase in B.A. starting salary for teachers.

[b]CD = number of comparable districts with lower starting salaries for teachers in autumn of previous year.

[c]Not enough information was available to determine these amounts.

[d]The 1955 state legislature stayed in session until 1956, when it was decided to grant $400 in salary increases in the following manner: $200 starting September 1956, $100 starting September 1957, and $100 starting September 1958.

[e]The state's action changed increments only and thus had no effect on starting salaries.

tively small appropriations, they were disregarded in order to concentrate on the study of general salary increases.

The information in Table 14 reveals that a general salary increase may arise in either of two ways. First, the legislature may raise the state-wide minimums on teachers' salaries. If the district is affected (as it was in the 1957 and 1964 budgets), it will usually receive offsetting revenues. The decision to grant raises to other employees at the same time arises out of an organizational norm for equitable treatment and is not associated with compensating funds. In the model the state's decision is treated as an external shock which necessarily leads to commensurate adjustments for all other personnel.

The second type of general increase is initiated by the school system and has occurred in the 1954, 1956, 1960, and 1962 budgets. Interviews revealed that the impetus for this move is the desire to adjust teachers' salaries and that, as before, other personnel enjoy raises in order to insure equitable treatment. Consequently, it is obvious that the most crucial decision to study is the district's determination to raise teachers' salaries.

In order to accomplish this it is necessary to provide some background information. As of 1965 most teachers belonged either to an affiliate of the National Education Association or to a local independent organization, while a small fraction were associated with the American Federation of Teachers. According to Wesley A. Wildman's classification of public bargaining relationships, the pattern here is one of "solicitation of views."[3] In other words, there is no formal bargaining agreement with the school system, but opinions are sought formally at an annual public meeting and informally by means of private consultations.

Teachers are paid according to a single salary schedule. Basically, the schedule is a matrix whose columns (teaching certificate, bachelor's degree, master's degree, master's degree plus 30 credits, master's degree plus 60 credits, and doctorate) represent academic background and whose fourteen rows represent number of years of teaching experience. A teacher with more academic background than another with the same number of years experience receives more pay, and a teacher with more years experience than another with the same academic background also receives more. Each year all teachers move from one row in the schedule to the next and obtain their automatic increment.

The state affects the schedule by imposing minimum values on the salaries in the matrix. For example, as of 1963 a teacher with

[3] Wesley A. Wildman, "Collective Action by Public School Teachers," *Industrial and Labor Relations Review,* 18, no. 1 (October, 1964): 8.

a bachelor's degree must receive at least $4,500 to start and must get annual increments of at least $300 until a maximum of not lower than $6,300 is reached. For a master's degree the minimum and maximum must be at least $4,500 and $6,900. The district affects the schedule by increasing the magnitudes of the entries in the matrix and by changing the number of rows and columns.

The Timing of Salary Increases

In order to discover when the district chooses to grant raises to teachers, the information used in making such a decision was examined. Various kinds of salary-schedule comparisons with other districts predominate. To those who have studied wage determination in the private sector this finding should not be surprising; it is well known that employers in business firms make salary comparisons. As a basic personnel-administration text documents: "Wages paid for comparable work by other firms in the labor market or in the industry may be the most important single factor in determining the ceiling of a firm's general wage level."[4]

There are a number of reasons why the district's administrators rely upon comparisons. Because of problems encountered in developing adequate measures, for example, there is little opportunity for school officials to base salary increases on such objective factors as productivity. With rational standards unavailable, organizations often turn to social criteria for making decisions; that is, current outcomes are judged good or bad by their proximity to those of similar organizations. Specifically, the efficacy of the current salary level is evaluated in terms of its relation to the levels of similar districts.[5]

[4] Paul Pigors and Charles A. Myers, *Personnel Administration,* 4th ed. (New York: McGraw-Hill, 1961), p. 366.

[5] This tactic is similar to that used by business firms in allocating funds to research and development units, since their contributions cannot readily be evaluated. For example, N. E. Seeber has found that firms tend to adopt some percentage of sales as a guide in R&D allocations and that the specific

Salary comparisons are also useful to school officials in dealing with the twin problems of recruitment of new teachers and retention of employed ones. According to Charles S. Benson the salary schedule is the only factor of importance to prospective teachers that can be adjusted in the short run.[6] Once competitive districts begin to raise their schedules an immediate response is necessary to avoid losing high-quality individuals. This produces a situation in which the continuous monitoring of salary data is necessary, especially when a general increase has not been granted for some time.

Salary levels can be rank-ordered to distinguish one district from another and are readily visible owing to the published reports of such organizations as the National Education Association. They therefore qualify as a dimension along which status can be measured. As a result, school administrators watch their relative salary position closely in order to guard against falling into an incongruent state.

Not only school officials, but also teachers make salary comparisons.[7] In preparing recommendations for the 1963 budget, for example, the salary committee of the local teachers association in the model's district made a study of thirty-eight comparable systems. Of significance for administrators in the analysis of such information by employees is that it has the potential for adversely affecting morale. In particular, teachers might be expected to react

figure is influenced by estimates of the percentage of sales used by similar organizations. His research is discussed in Richard M. Cyert and James G. March, *A Behavioral Theory of the Firm* (Englewood Cliffs, N.J.: Prentice-Hall, 1963), pp. 274–275. Along the same general lines, Leon Festinger has observed in "A Theory of Social Comparison Processes," in *Small Groups: Studies in Social Interaction,* ed. A. Paul Hare, Edgar F. Borgatta, and Robert F. Bales (New York: Alfred A. Knopf, 1955), pp. 163–186, that when objective means are unavailable, individuals seek to evaluate their opinions on a certain issue by comparison with those who tend to have similar views.

[6] Benson, *Economics of Public Education,* pp. 420–421.

[7] Benson, *ibid.,* p. 418, has noted that the typical rationale behind teachers' requests for increases is the level of salaries in similar districts.

unfavorably toward comparisons which reveal that their counterparts in similar districts are receiving higher pay, since one of the basic laws of "social justice" holds that unless the rewards of individuals with similar characteristics are equal, the one who is relatively deprived will be dissatisfied. While it seems that this has not been empirically verified in the case of teachers, evidence has been supplied that blue-collar workers who have relatively low wages tend to choose as comparisons those who are earning more and have similar status. Moreover, it has been found that such dissonant comparisons breed dissatisfaction in the persons who make them.[8] Accordingly, it would be expected that one way in which school administrators might keep track of the discontent of teachers is by referring to salary comparisons themselves.

In order to observe the precise manner in which salary information influences the timing decision, further explanation is needed. To make the task less formidable it was necessary to select from the many types of comparisons that can be made a single one which is particularly significant. The relationship of the starting salary for teachers with a bachelor's degree (the B.A. minimum) to that of other districts seems to meet this requirement. It is certainly influential for recruitment purposes, since most new teachers are hired directly from college, and it also serves as a measure of the discontent of presently employed teachers and of the status of the school system (to the extent to which it indicates the position of the entire schedule relative to others).

Decision-making was not so refined that the persons interviewed could pinpoint the comparable districts in any given year. Nevertheless, they did feel that the salaries of the large districts in the northeastern section of the country had the most influence on them. This may seem a rather surprising observation since it implies that the market for teachers is regional rather than local in nature.

[8] See George Caspar Homans, *Social Behavior: Its Elementary Forms* (New York: Harcourt, Brace and World, 1961), pp. 72–78; and Martin Patchen, *The Choice of Wage Comparisons* (Englewood Cliffs, N.J.: Prentice-Hall, 1961), Chap. 5.

A possible explanation is that in keeping pace with the other large systems the district at the same time keeps ahead of its suburbs. An effort was made to test this hypothesis, but the necessary data could not be obtained.

By operationally defining the criteria supplied in the interviews, a list of districts was developed which it was believed would contain the essential ones. Only those urban—as opposed to county—districts with enrollment of at least 50,000 pupils in the 1964/65 school year and in the northeastern quadrant of the nation were selected as being comparable.[9] Using information published by the Research Division of the National Education Association, it was possible to compile B.A. minimums for all the selected districts from the 1953/54 school year to the 1964/65 school year.[10] To be useful these data must represent the situation just before the model's system makes its decision in a given year, which, as explained previously, occurs in the last quarter. This appears to be true, since each set of yearly information is dated September, October, or November and the district's salary is always the pre-increase figure. Initial review of the data revealed that two districts, one in Kentucky and the other in West Virginia, had the lowest B.A. minimums in all years. Since they appeared not to be in competition with the other cities, they were removed from consideration. The remaining eighteen cities, including the model's, make up the com-

---

[9] The northeastern quadrant comprises the states northeast of and including Wisconsin, Illinois, Kentucky, West Virginia, and Virginia.

[10] The data for the 1962/63 to 1964/65 school years were obtained from National Education Association, Research Division, *Salary Schedules, Classroom Teachers, Districts having 3,000 or More Pupils* (Washington, D.C.: The Association, 1962–1964). For 1957/58 to 1961/62 the source was NEA, *Salary Schedules, Classroom Teachers, Urban Districts 100,000 and Over in Population* (Washington, D.C.: The Association, 1957–1961). The data for 1953/54, 1955/56, and 1956/57 are from Cincinnati Public Schools, Research Department, "Reports on Salary Structure of Cities over 200,000 in Population," mimeographed (Cincinnati, Ohio: The Department, 1953, 1955, 1956). Finally, the 1954/55 information was obtained from NEA, *Teachers Salary Schedules in 125 Urban School Districts over 100,000 in Population* (Washington, D.C.: The Association, 1954).

parison list. Their salary history is shown in Appendix III.

For each year the number of districts whose B.A. minimum was below, the same as, and above the model's was determined. The first quantity is found in Table 14 as *CD*. A general salary increase was initiated by the district when and only when no other system had a lower B.A. minimum. This correspondence occurred four times: in the 1954, 1956, 1960, and 1962 budgets. On these occasions the number of other systems that had the same minimum salary was only 5, 3, 2, and 1, respectively. The district was always in last place before action was taken, a finding which corresponds to the statement of one old-timer who said, "Everytime we get to the bottom of the list we grant an increase." This evidence prompted the formulation of the following decision rule:

> *Rule 5:* Grant a general salary increase when no comparable school districts have lower B.A. starting salaries for teachers.

Before leaving the subject of timing an important implication of the results needs to be discussed. An organizational wage structure which is similar in many respects to that which has been hypothesized for the business firm by John T. Dunlop seems to have been discovered.[11] In his theory environmental influences cause adjustments in the wage rate of a "key" occupation which are then transmitted to other, similar rates in a job cluster. Apparently, in the model's district the teacher's salary is the key rate, because environmental factors, namely salary levels in similar organizations, lead to its change and as a result to changes for other occupations.

Of great significance for the further development of the ideas presented in this section is Dunlop's concept of a wage contour. He has hypothesized that job-cluster rates in firms with similar products will move together because of the linkages between their key rates. If it is mechanistically assumed that pupils are the "product" of school systems, then it is possible to argue that the salaries

---

[11] John T. Dunlop, "The Task of Contemporary Wage Theory," in *New Concepts in Wage Determination,* ed. George W. Taylor and Frank C. Pierson (New York: McGraw-Hill, 1957), pp. 117–139.

of the districts listed in Appendix III are part of a wage contour. This would be the case if each of the other systems made its salary choices in the same manner as the model's; that is, by means of a comparison process involving all the other districts. On the surface such a conclusion seems unlikely because in a number of these cities a formal bargaining relationship exists between the district and either the A.F.T. or N.E.A. affiliate. But this objection can be answered by pointing out that, at least in the private sector, the salary-comparison phenomenon may actually be intensified when unions enter the picture because of competition among rival employee groups.[12]

Unfortunately, the data in Appendix III are not suitable in their present form for testing the wage-contour hypothesis. Increases initiated by each state must first be separated out, and the data adjusted for systems that do not make their decisions in the fall. If further research led to verification, however, a simulation model could be designed which would predict the future time path of salary increases in the major northeastern public school systems.

The Amount of Salary Increase

It has been implied that a general salary increase will be granted whether financial resources are expected to be abundant or lean, since the only important criterion is the number of comparable districts with lower B.A. starting salaries for teachers. Indeed, in the 1954 budget a general raise was provided even though a deficit was forecast without its inclusion. Also, large amounts of excess funds were available for distribution in the 1958 and 1965 budgets, but no general increase was given. Yet on an intuitive basis it would be surprising if ability to pay did not somehow enter in as a crucial factor. In order to understand the manner in which these two criteria are reconciled when they conflict, it is necessary to consider

---

[12] Arthur M. Ross, *Trade Union Wage Policy* (Berkeley, Calif.: University of California Press, 1948), p. 49.

once again the role of the state legislature in the decision process.

The legislature meets every odd year to allocate educational funds for the following two years to local districts. The prevailing pattern has been for the model's system to receive a sizeable revenue increase on each of these occasions. This represents the district's only major source of added funds, since it has consistently remained at the limit of its power to raise tax rates or institute new levies. Therefore, the administration expects that the budget for an even year (prepared during an odd year) will have sizeable added revenues unless evidence to the contrary is available. Similarly, it is expected that the budget for an odd year (prepared in an even year) will not contain much additional funds unless evidence to the contrary is on hand.

The result is a process in which the amount of increase in the B.A. starting salary is chosen so that some comparable districts will have lower starting salaries until the next expected opportunity for the district to receive a large increase in revenues. Typically, the raise is such that enough is provided for an even budget year to keep the system from the bottom of the comparison list until two years hence. Thus, in the 1960 budget the B.A. minimum was raised $300; an increase was not required again until the 1962 budget. In the exceptional case where it is known that added funds will not be forthcoming from the next session of the legislature, the amount is larger. For example, in preparing the 1962 budget, it appeared that nothing could be expected from the 1963 legislature.[13] Accordingly, the B.A. starting salary was raised $700, an amount which it could be anticipated would prevent the need for a raise until the 1966 budget.

The reason for providing two "normal" increases in starting salaries in the 1962 budget as opposed to one for 1962 and another for 1964 stems from a reluctance to test legal rulings against planned

---

[13] The 1961 legislature increased the district's revenues on the condition that unless an emergency arose there would be no additional funds granted by the next session in 1963. However, there was an emergency associated with the 1963 budget which led the next session to provide a temporary increase in the millage rate.

surpluses. Suppose that during the 1962 budget preparation the system adopted the latter course of action. Then the funds available for the extra increase would have been allocated to other expenditure categories rather than being reserved for 1964 increases. Since revenues for 1964 were anticipated to be about the same as for 1962, they would just about cover only previously made expenditure commitments. Accordingly, there could be no unallocated funds available for the 1964 salary increase.

There is no information to serve as a guide in determining the amount of increase in the B.A. minimum which might be granted when the budget is being prepared for an odd year. Over the time period examined, $t+1$ has never been odd when $CD = 0$. Hence, this path was excluded from consideration in the model.

When additional revenues are expected from the next session of the legislature, the increase in the other entries of the teachers' schedule are usually equal in magnitude to the raise in the B.A. minimum. This policy is followed in the model where the 1960 budget figure of $300 is used for all teachers. When added funds are not expected from the next legislature, the raise in the B.A. minimum and in other teachers' salaries may not be equal. In the 1962 budget the B.A. minimum was raised $700, but other teachers' salaries were raised in varying amounts from $300 to $700. To handle this type of situation in the model the 1962 average increase for teachers ($425) is used for all teachers. The amounts granted simultaneously to the other occupational groups were not analyzed, owing to a lack of data. The interviewees felt, however, that these individuals enjoyed commensurate increases. In the model it was assumed that on the average all other employees receive the same increases as teachers.

Debt Service on New Bond Issues

Another important long-term commitment is the budgeting of debt service on "new" bonds—those bonds for which the initial debt service payment will appear in the budget for $t+1$. Even though bonds actually issued in the first half of t may meet this criterion, they are considered given in the model because these decisions are made prior to budget preparation for $t+1$. Only new bonds whose issuance is still subject to discretion during budget preparation will be examined. Whether or not these bonds are ever actually issued is immaterial; it is only their effect on the operating budget which is of interest.

The district's policy is to issue general obligation bonds, maturing in twenty-five years. They bear equal principal payments at the end of each year and annual interest payments in six-month installments. As a result of these regulations, there are four ways in which debt service on a new bond issue may be planned for in the coming year's budget. It is possible, of course, to do nothing. More direct action may be taken by issuing bonds in the second half of the coming year. In both cases the coming year's budget is unaffected. Bonds may also be planned for the first half of the next year, in which case the new budget must contain an added provision for one interest payment. Finally, it can be decided to issue bonds before the end of the present year. This decision must lead to an appropriation of one principal payment and two interest payments in the coming budget.

The decision on which of these alternatives to adopt is affected by the current state of the bond fund. It is conditioned, for example, by how much money is owed on contracts let for the construction of capital projects and by whether such alternative methods of financing capital projects as taking temporary bank loans or using temporarily idle cash in other funds must be repaid. When the value of let contracts is high and alternative methods of financing are exhausted and must be paid back, it is time to consider the possibility of a new bond issue.[14] Therefore, to a large extent bonds

---

[14] Another factor is the expectations of interest rate trends. If rates are estimated to be higher in the first half of next year than in the second half, for example, an issue may be planned for the latter period. The necessary information on interest rate expectations was unavailable, however, so this factor cannot be considered in the model. As will be seen, it has not been crucial in the recent past.

Table 15—New Debt Service

Budget	Item	Principal	Interest	WC^a
1956	—	$ 0	$ 0	$1,863,533
1957	Loan	0	15,000	180,487
1958	Loan	0	35,000	−1,521,985
1959	Loan	0	30,000	585,911
1960	Loan 1959 bonds 1960 bonds	241,170 120,000 0	30,000 105,000 37,000	−3,369,736
1961	Loan	0	30,000	−1,891,494
1962	Loan 1962 bonds	0 0	30,000 87,500	−3,407,932
1963	Loan	0	15,000	−676,028
1964	Loan 1963 bonds	0 200,000	15,000 156,250	−3,934,070
1965	Loan	0	15,000	−946,876

aWorking capital of bond fund on August 31 of the previous year.

are used to pay for past obligations rather than to implement plans for the future. When the pressure of these financial obligations gets high, it is to be expected that a bond issue would be planned for the beginning of the next year. If such pressures become acute during budget preparation, a bond issue would be planned for the current year. In the remaining part of the section these theories will be made operational.

Normally the chief accountant has had a great deal of influence in deciding whether or not to budget new bonds. The current holder of the office revealed that because of the preferences of his predecessor, prior to the 1956 budget the organization utilized decision rules different from those followed at present. Since he could not remember the nature of the old rules in detail, analysis begins with the 1956 budget and continues up to the 1965 budget, which is the last one studied. Table 15 reveals that over this time period debt service on new bonds appeared in the 1960, 1962, and 1964 budgets.

In order to develop a measure of financial pressure which can predict the budgeting of new bonds, an attempt was made to discover the information analyzed in coming to a decision. This information involves the estimation of the amount of funds that will be available for financing capital projects in the near future. It was not possible to obtain the data, however, since they were considered confidential. As a result, the monthly balance sheets for the bond fund were used. A pressure measure was obtained by calculating for each August 31 statement a figure which will be called working capital, although strictly speaking there are some minor differences between the two.[15] This date was chosen because it comes before those bonds which have been budgeted to appear in the second half of t and at the same time is late enough so that the information it contains is pertinent for decision-making purposes. The data used in the calculations are shown in Appendix III.

An analysis of the past relationship between the value of working capital and the budgeting of new debt service can be made by referring to Table 15. The measure is able to discriminate between the conditions of no new debt service and some new debt service. Corresponding to the provisions for new debt service which appear in the 1960, 1962, and 1964 budgets are working-capital figures which are well below the figures in other years. For example, the difference between the highest in the first group (1960) and the lowest in the second (1961) is about $1,500,000.

The measure has some difficulty, however, in distinguishing between the need to issue bonds at the beginning of the next year and the end of this year. Thus, the data for the 1962 and 1964 budgets are consistent with the aforementioned theories, but the data for

[15] The current liabilities used in my calculations include contracts awarded for the construction of capital projects; some of this amount may not have to be paid until more than a year has passed. I also included encumbrances, which represent purchase orders, as a current liability, although the school system does not. Removing encumbrances from consideration does not affect the results. The source of the information used in calculating the financial pressure measure was Pittsburgh Board of Public Education, "Combined Balance Sheet for the Month Ending August 31, Exhibit 'A,' " *Minutes of the Board of Public Education,* 45 (1955/56)–54 (1964/65).

the 1960 budget are not. While preparing the 1964 budget, a $5,000,000 bond issue was planned for the end of 1963. Working capital attained its lowest value at this time. When a $5,000,000 issue was planned for the beginning of 1962, working capital was at its second-lowest value. While preparing the 1960 budget, a $3,000,000 issue was planned for the end of 1959 and a $2,000,-000 issue for the beginning of 1960. Presumably, this was done because the pressures for an immediate $5,000,000 issue were not great. Therefore, some of it could be delayed to take advantage of what was thought to be more favorable interest rates later. Accordingly, it would be expected that the working-capital figure corresponding to the 1960 budget would be between the 1962 and 1964 figures. Actually, however, it is just above the 1962 figure.[16]

In the model new debt service is predicted according to a rule which uses two parameters (P_A and P_B) as boundaries to define regions of financial pressure within which differing actions are appropriate:

> *Rule 6:* If the working capital of the bond fund at the end of August is less than or equal to $P_A (P_A < 0)$, then budget for bonds to be issued at the end of the current year. If working capital is less than or equal to $P_B (P_A < P_B < 0)$ but larger than P_A, then budget for bonds to be issued in the first half of next year. If working capital is greater than P_B, do not budget for new bonds.

After examining the data in Table 15, $-3,500,000 was chosen

---

[16] It might have been argued that the value of working capital was in line for 1960 and 1964 and too low for 1962. However, at the end of 1958 a controversy between the building inspection bureau of the municipal government and the school system erupted over fire safety standards in the school buildings. At the end of April 1959, the school system received official notification of what had to be done to improve standards. It is unlikely that all contracts for this work could have been let by August 31, which is the date of the working-capital figure. Therefore, expectations that more contracts would be let in the immediate future for this purpose probably influenced the decision on new debt service. Hence, the magnitude of the figure undoubtedly understates the appropriate one.

for the value of P_A. Any value between $-3,407,932$ and $-3,934,070$ could have been chosen without changing the predictions. The value of P_B was set at $-2,500,000$. Here, any value between $-1,891,494$ and $-3,369,736$ might have been selected without affecting predictions.

As an alternative to Rule 6 a prediction which would schedule new debt service only in budgets for even-numbered years might be considered. Such a rule would, however, incorrectly predict the presence of new debt service in the 1956 and 1958 budgets, while Rule 6 would correctly predict no such occurrence. Yet all three instances of new debt service have occurred in even-year budgets. It therefore seems likely that when financial pressure builds up and new bonds will soon have to be issued, an effort will be made to control this pressure so that the bonds will appear in relatively abundant years.

The Amount of New Debt Service

In order to determine the amount of new debt service to budget in the model, parameters were chosen in the following manner: First, $5,000,000 was chosen as the amount of the typical issue, since all the recent bonds were of this amount (considering the 1959 and 1960 issues as one). Then an interest rate of 3.5 percent was selected because it is currently used by the staff. Using these figures, it can be determined that $375,000 will be budgeted if working capital $\leq$ $-3,500,000$; a principal payment of $5,000,000/25 = $200,000 and an interest payment of $5,000,000 \times 0.035 = $175,000, will be introduced into the coming budget. If working capital is $\leq$ $-2,500,000$ and $>$ $-3,500,000$, then $87,500 will be appropriated. In this case, only one semiannual interest payment needs to be allocated: $($5,000,000 \times 0.035)/2 = $87,500.

An examination of Table 15 will also reveal that every budget since 1957 has had a provision for interest on temporary loans as a precaution. These loans usually pay for capital projects or finance operating expenses if the state appropriation payment is delayed. In the model, the current allocation of $15,000 is used. The table also shows a principal payment on a loan in the 1960 budget. The amount represents a deficit incurred in 1959 which was made up with borrowed funds. This decision could have easily been incorporated into the model but was not because it was an isolated instance.

Explanation of Charts 3 and 4

Recent work on the subject of organizational decision-making has analyzed the topic from a pressure point of view. In other words, it has been assumed that administrators react to short-run feedback information rather than develop plans based on long-run predictions. A case in point is the theory of the decision process formulated by Richard M. Cyert and James G. March, an approach also characterizing the simulation model of a hypothetical firm developed by Charles P. Bonini.[17] Bonini assumes that each person in the firm has an "index of felt pressure," which consists of a weighted average of his reaction to accounting information and the pressure passed on to him by his supervisor. The magnitude of an individual's index determines his decision-making. Thus, when it has a high value, foremen cut costs, supervisors spend more time supervising, and salesmen sell more or less, depending upon their personalities.[18]

It appears that the same type of general process characterizes the salary-increase and new debt-service decisions in the model's school system. Salary-comparison and working-capital data may be looked upon as short-run feedback information which serves as the basis for pressure indices developed by the staff. In the former case pressure is due to morale, recruitment, and status considerations, while in the latter it arises from the need to meet previously

[17] Cyert and March, *Behavioral Theory,* pp. 114–127; and Charles P. Bonini, *Simulation of Information and Decision Systems in the Firm* (Englewood Cliffs, N.J.: Prentice-Hall, 1963).
[18] Bonini, *Simulation of Information,* pp. 54–68.

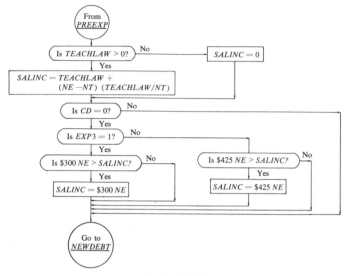

Chart 3. *SALINC*

made financial commitments. As the number of comparable districts with lower B.A. minimums approaches zero and working capital becomes highly negative, pressure begins to develop for a decision to correct the situation. When these two types of information reach critical values, the magnitude of the resulting pressure leads to a general raise and new bonds.

It is now possible to transform these theories on general salary increases and new debt service into a more rigorous format. A flow diagram for the salary decision appears in Chart 3. The model first inquires into the amount the state has provided in salary increases for teachers (*TEACHLAW*). If the state has provided nothing, the amount of salary increase in the coming budget (*SALINC*) is temporarily set equal to zero. If the state has acted, then *SALINC* is temporarily set equal to *TEACHLAW* plus a commensurate raise for other employees. The commensurate-raise component is determined by multiplying the average mandated increase per teacher (*TEACHLAW/NT*) by the number of other personnel

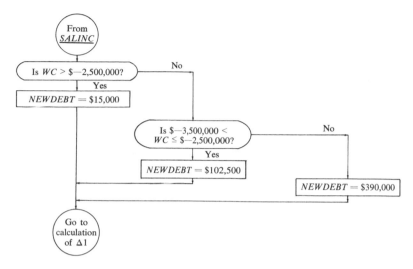

Chart 4. *NEWDEBT*

$(NE - NT)$. Here, NE is the total number of employees and NT is the number of teachers.

Next an inquiry is made into whether or not the number of comparable districts with B.A. minimum salaries below the model's (CD) is equal to zero. If not, the existing value of $SALINC$ goes into the budget. If so, a general salary increase will be provided by the district and the total amount must be determined.

As a result, it must be discovered whether or not added funds are expected for $t+3$ $(EXP\,3)$. Using the assumption that $t+1$ is always an even year when $CD = 0$, the value of $EXP\,3$ can be found in the following manner: Added funds will not be expected for $t+3$ $(EXP\,3 = 0)$ if it is currently known that the next legislature will not provide them. Additional revenues will be expected for $t+3$ $(EXP\,3 = 1)$ otherwise, since normally it is believed that the next legislature will provide enough to finance a salary increase at that time. In short, it is reasonable to assume that there will either be enough for a general raise or that there will be nothing.

If added funds are expected, the staff will compare the increase arising from state regulations (the existing value of *SALINC*) to the general raise it is willing to provide in this situation ($300 × *NE*). If the general raise is larger, then it will be budgeted, but if, on the other hand, the state-induced raise is larger, it will be budgeted. In this way the state increase is incorporated into the general raise and vice versa.

If added funds are not expected in $t+3$, then the same process is followed as when they are, but $425 replaces $300 in the board's calculations. Then the model moves on to consider any new debt service (the *NEWDEBT* process).

The flow diagram for the new debt-service decision appears in Chart 4. A check is made first to see whether working capital (*WC*) > $−2,500,000. If so, then the only new debt-service provision (*NEWDEBT*) is $15,000 for interest on a temporary loan. If working capital is ≤ $−2,500,000 and > $−3,500,000, then $102,500 is budgeted for one semiannual interest payment on bonds to be issued at the beginning of the next year and for interest on a temporary loan. Finally, if working capital ≤ $−3,500,000, then *NEWDEBT* equals $390,000. This includes one principal payment and two interest payments on a bond issue scheduled for the end of the current year. It also includes interest on a temporary loan. At this point the model proceeds to the calculation of the projected surplus or deficit for $t+1$ (Δ 1).

5
Balancing the Budget

Once the decisions concerning preliminary major-subunit allocations and long-run commitments have been made, the model, as
demonstrated in Chart 1, calculates the surplus or deficit for
$t+1$. When preliminary expenditures exceed forecasted revenues
($\Delta 1 < 0$), the process labeled *SEARCH* is activated to remove
the deficit. If forecasted revenues are greater than or equal to
preliminary spending ($\Delta 1 \geq 0$), it is necessary to distribute any
surplus, using the *SLACK* process.

The Deficit-Removal Process

There have been three budgets from 1954 to 1965 in which
preliminary spending exceeded forecasted revenues (1954, 1959,
1963). In addition, there have been two other budgets (1960,
1962) in which a projected surplus was intentionally increased to
make room for certain new appropriations. The model has no
mechanism for predicting when the latter situation will arise; this
is one area in which the simulation could be refined. Meanwhile,
since there is no reason to believe that the rules for enlarging a
surplus are substantially different from those for eliminating a
deficit, the data for 1960 and 1962 were used to help explain the
budgetary cuts in 1954, 1959, and 1963. From these data and the
interviews a set of budget-cutting procedures (whose main features
are discussed below) was developed.

The model's deficit-removal process, which is labeled *SEARCH,* begins with a review of the preliminarily budgeted value of the provision for unexpended appropriations (PUA). A deduction on the expenditure side of the budget, PUA is used because not all appropriations are normally spent. The preliminary value is predicted using the amount budgeted for t.

As long as the provision for unexpended appropriations remains less than actual cancelled appropriations, it can be used to decrease budgeted spending without affecting actual spending. If its value turns out to be greater than cancellations, actual spending will exceed budgeted spending. Since this condition violates state regulations, actual spending will have to be reduced. Accordingly, PUA's magnitude will be increased to a point which represents an estimate of the amount of actual cancellations in $t+1$. This upper limit is predicted in the model by the highest budgeted value of PUA over the years investigated ($405,000 in the 1962 budget). This choice is supported by the fact that the budget for the following year was the only one in which a deficit existed and the provision was not increased. The following rule is the result:

> *Rule 7A:* If a deficit is projected, increase the provision for unexpended appropriations by either $405,000 minus its preliminary value or by the magnitude of the deficit, whichever is smaller.

After this step, either of two different methods may be used to balance the budget. The first (Process 1) cuts budgeted expenditures, while the second (Process 2) consists of raising revenue forecasts to levels whose chances of occurring are lower than usual, yet not unrealistic.

The staff's expectations of added funds for the year after the next $(t+2)$ determine which of these mechanisms will be used. Process 1 will be utilized if added funds are not expected for $t+2$, since the deficit would continue into that year if not eliminated. In the model this condition exists provided $t+2$ is odd (with the exception noted below), since added funds are not usually expected in such a year.

Process 1 will also be used if $t+2$ is even and it is known that the next legislature will not be providing added funds for that year. Process 2 will be called into play if it is expected that sufficient funds will be available in $t+2$ to absorb the next year's deficit. Then, provided the revenue forecasts for $t+1$ prove to be realistic, budgetary cuts will not have to be made in the near future. In the model sufficient funds are expected if $t+2$ is even (with the exception noted above), since the next legislature will usually provide added funds for such a year. Process 2 will also be used if $t+2$ is odd, provided it is known that the current legislature has allocated funds which cannot be used until $t+2$. In predicting expectations for $t+2$ it is reasonable to assume that there will be enough added to cover the deficit or that nothing will be added.

In developing the content of Process 2 it is sufficient to provide that any remaining deficit, after the provision for unexpended appropriations is used, will be eliminated by reinvestigating revenue forecasts. No further detail is necessary since budgeted spending and, therefore, the model's predictions are not affected by its use. While this argument implicitly assumes that forecasts can remain realistic and at the same time eliminate any deficit, it does not appear to be contradicted by the available data. If a deficit should arise which could not be completely eliminated by Process 2, it seems plausible that attention would turn to Process 1. This refinement can easily be introduced into the model.

If expectations dictate the use of Process 1 instead of Process 2, the next step involves the transfer of capital-outlay appropriations from the operating budget to the capital budget. Preliminarily, these allocations find their way into the operating budget in order to save interest costs. A transfer back to the capital budget, while changing the source from which the funds are provided, does not lower actual spending for operations. The particular account which is affected by the transfer is the alterations component of the school buildings appropriation, which is assigned number 30140 in the budget. Its suitability derives from its large size and its resemblance to typical capital budget outlays. Accordingly, the rule is:

> *Rule 7B:* If a deficit remains, decrease account 30140 by either its preliminary appropriation or the magnitude of the remaining deficit, whichever is smaller.

From this point on, any reductions in budgeted spending will unavoidably lead to cuts in actual spending. The particular areas that the model examines first are noneducational services and educational services outside the regular day school program. Since the district does not classify the activities that should belong to these two groups, it was not easy to determine their composition. In addition, there are some activities, such as kindergarten, whose inclusion or exclusion could both be convincingly argued. Recognizing that a certain degree of arbitrariness must enter into the choices, pupil services, school health, custodians for the public use of buildings, summer recreation, and summer gardens were chosen to constitute the noneducational group; and the extension education office, summer schools, evening schools, and nursery schools were selected for the second category. Of these, the summer recreation program, summer gardens, and nursery schools are not currently provided, but were offered sometime during the period from 1954 to 1965.

The model makes reductions only in the preliminary personnel appropriations of the "fringe" services listed above, since preliminary materials allocations are typically very small. The preliminary personnel outlays are only for employees on hand at the start of budget preparation and are not for any new personnel, because fringe activities are part of the miscellaneous spending category for which the new-personnel component is predicted to be zero. It was not possible to predict the limit to which the personnel allocations of each service would be cut. Undoubtedly, a lower limit determined by functions required by state law exists, but mandated and nonmandated outlays could not be separated. Predictions for any particular year are made by aggregating the appropriations for the existing personnel of each service and reducing the sum by a given percentage. This figure, representing the amount eliminated divided by the total amount, was calculated for the two budgets in which fringe services were reduced in order to cut a deficit. Its value was 32 percent in the 1954 budget and 7 percent in the 1963 budget. The difference in size between the two suggests that they are not from the same distribution. This seems likely because of the changes in administrative personnel and policy which took place over the nine-year period separating the two budgets. Consequently, the more recent figure was used in the model. The corresponding rule is:

> *Rule 7C:* If a deficit still exists, reduce the preliminary personnel appropriations for the fringe services by either 7 percent or a percentage which will eliminate the deficit, whichever is smaller.

As the next step in the process the major subunits will be examined. It is assumed that an effort will be made to treat all of these accounts equally regardless of their priority. First, new personnel added during the initial review will be removed, but no existing employees will be affected. Since no new employees can be budgeted unless the G.I.M. is high, this policy is not likely to be very fruitful. Next, there will be cuts in the major subunits' materials accounts. Here a rule is employed which reduces each appropriation by a fixed percentage. In order to estimate this figure, the district's budgetary history was examined. For 1954, differing percentage cuts were made in all supply, repair and replacement, and capital-outlay accounts in the budget. For 1963, supplies of the major subunits in the second and third priorities were cut 10 percent, while texts and school-room supplies were cut by less than 10 percent. Evidently the rule is not an exact replica of the decision process in either year, but represents an attempt to capture important aspects of both cuts. As a result, there is no data from which to directly estimate the percentage. The problem was handled by assuming that the total amount cut from the major subunits for 1963 represented a maximum amount, since on top of cuts in expenditures, the system had to resort to the use of nonrecurring revenues. The maximum amount corresponds to a 5 percent cut in total major-subunit materials appropriations and is the figure used in the model.

The rules for the major subunits are:

> *Rule 7D:* If a deficit is still projected, reduce each major-subunit new-personnel account by a percentage which overall will eliminate the remaining deficit or by the preliminarily approved appropriation, whichever is smaller.
>
> *Rule 7E:* Then, if necessary, reduce each major-subunit materials appropriation by a percentage which overall will eliminate the remaining deficit or by 5 percent, whichever is smaller.

In the final step of the process it is assumed that all possible reductions in budgeted expenditures have been made. The school system must use methods which affect the revenue side of the budget. Examples include the use of nonrecurring revenues or perhaps the reinvestigation of revenue forecasts. Since budgeted spending is not affected, it is not necessary to model these methods in detail. Thus, the last rule is:

> *Rule 7F:* If a deficit remains at this point, balance the budget by increasing budgeted revenues.

The overall process involves the use of relatively simple rules in a step-by-step fashion. The initial rules are chosen because they contribute toward balancing the budget without affecting actual spending. There may be an increase in the provision for unexpended appropriations, a reinvestigation of the revenue forecasts, and a transfer of capital-outlay appropriations to the bond fund. If these strategies fail, it becomes necessary to make decisions which will limit actual expenditures. There is a search of vulnerable areas in the budget. Reductions are made in noneducational services presumably because their benefits are only indirectly linked to educational goals. Cuts are also made in educational services outside the regular day school program, perhaps because they affect relatively small segments of the student population. These cuts may not be made, however, without adverse affects. There are indications that a price in status may have to be paid, since the ability to provide fringe services is a characteristic of major school systems. It is only after these activities are reviewed that attention is focused on the major subunits. As a last resort, when no further reductions can be made in spending, the budget must be balanced by reexamining revenues.[1]

A Comparison of Actual and Predicted Reductions

It would be unfair to imply that the actual process for reducing deficits is as clearly defined as the one portrayed in the model. Differences exist from year to year, the causes of which cannot easily be incorporated into a highly structured framework. For example, the mere fact that nine years separate the first and last occasions for the removal of a deficit means that changes in administrative personnel are likely to affect decision-making policy. On the other hand, data analysis revealed that a crude pattern did seem to exist, and the interviews corroborated this observation. Thus, it was learned from those responsible for making cuts in the 1963 budget that they examined the 1954 reductions in order to get ideas.

---

[1] The structure of the deficit-removal routine appears to conform in a number of ways to the concept of a search process developed by James G. March and Herbert A. Simon in *Organizations* (New York: John Wiley, 1958), Chaps. 6 and 7. The model's routine consists of two performance programs: the revenue-reinvestigation method and the expenditure-reduction method. The latter consists in turn of a set of standard operating rules and in some cases screening procedures for examining whether a particular rule can be used. An example of a screening procedure is the check to determine whether the current value of the provision for unexpended appropriations is less than the allowable limit. The routine also contains a higher-level switching rule for selecting the appropriate performance program to use in a specific instance. The switching rule is represented by the use to which expectations for the year after next are put.

Table 16—Comparison of Actual and Predicted Reductions

		1954		1959	
Rule	Item	Actual	Model	Actual	Model
7A	Provision	$ 250,000	$ 405,000	$155,000	$205,000
	Revenue reinvestigation	0	0	573,000	523,000
7B	Account 30140	0	50,000	0	0
7C	Fringe services	320,404	69,700	0	0
7D	Major-subunit new personnel	13,800	65,300	0	0
7E	Major-subunit materials	362,000	94,700	0	0
7F	Nonrecurring revenues	0	428,395	0	0
	Other	166,891	0	0	0
	Total deficit	$1,113,095	$1,113,095	$728,000	$728,000

By comparing the model's predictions with some actual situations, the reader should acquire some basis for judging the extent to which the model approaches reality. Table 16 presents a comparison of the model's reductions with actual reductions in the 1954, 1959, 1960, 1962, and 1963 budgets. In these calculations the actual amounts of all decisions prior to the removal of the deficit were used so that errors from other parts of the model would not confuse the results.

The comparison procedure is not as straightforward as might be thought, since there are a number of different comparisons which can be made. It seems reasonable that the budget areas upon which attention is focused, the order in which they are cut, and the amount taken from each area should be checked. The first check can be made by examining the "Other" row in Table 16, since it indicates the amount of the cuts in areas not considered by the deficit-removal process. For the most part, these areas have been used only in isolated instances or have not individually accounted for large reductions. In order to examine the situation in greater detail, the amount of other cuts as a percentage of the total deficit on a yearly basis was calculated. The figures are 15, 0, 17, 21, and 9 percent for the 1954 through 1963 budgets. In examining the

1960		1962		1963	
Actual	Model	Actual	Model	Actual	Model
$ 50,000	$140,000	$150,000	$150,000	$ 0	$ 100,000
0	0	0	513,000	0	0
425,000	425,000	374,000	0	450,000	450,000
0	10,000	0	0	81,864	81,864
0	0	0	0	15,000	12,000
0	0	0	0	94,934	94,934
0	0	0	0	700,000	729,557
100,000a	0	139,000	0	126,557	0
$575,000	$575,000	$663,000	$663,000	$1,468,355	$1,468,355

aThere are $350,000 more in other cuts, but only those presumably connected with the effort to increase the surplus are included here.

two years with the highest percentages, it turns out that of the 17 percent figure for the 1960 budget, an amount representing 12 percent of the total deficit is due to one item. In this case, funds for the alteration of secondary science laboratories were transferred from the operating budget to the capital budget. The essence of this procedure is already incorporated into the model as Rule 7B. The particular account is not part of that rule because it was affected only in the 1960 budget. It also appears that of the 21 percent figure for the 1962 budget, an amount representing 17 percent of the total deficit was due to reductions in sick leave and in the number of substitute teachers. This was the only year for which these accounts were cut; the reason for reduction could not be determined.

A comparison of the order in which cuts are made is not easy because there is little definite information on the order of actual reductions. An examination of Table 16 indicates, however, that Rules 7A and 7B are probably used first; they tend to appear whether large or small deficits are to be eliminated. The only exceptions are Rule 7A for 1963 and Rule 7B for 1954 (since

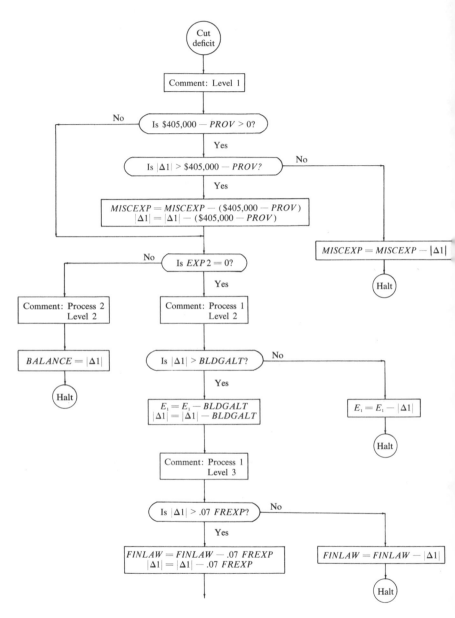

Chart 5. *SEARCH*

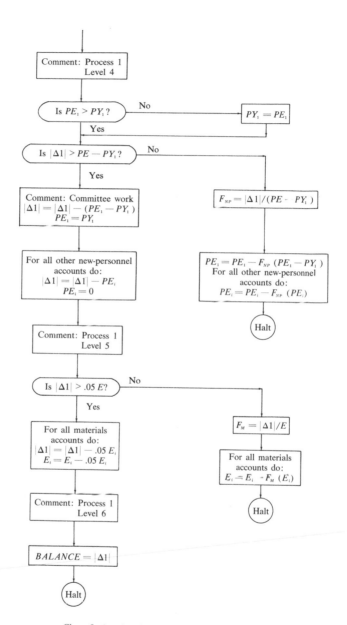

Chart 5 (continued)

account 30140 had not appeared in its present form by 1954). It was not possible to discover from Table 16 the order among Rules 7C, 7D, and 7E; the predicted arrangement is based on the views of the staff. Rule 7F appears to be a last resort because it was used only for the budget with the largest deficit.

In a final check large errors in the amounts of reductions were examined. Rule 7A's largest discrepancy occurs in 1954. It could not be learned why it occurred, but it was discovered that this was the first time the rule was used. The large errors in other years suggest that perhaps the rule's upper limit was selected too naively and that its value should have been based on actual cancellations in the recent past. The only serious deviation in the use of the revenue-reinvestigation process is for 1962; it was not possible to discover its cause. This error produces the only important discrepancy in the transfer of capital-outlay appropriations. The reductions in fringe benefits and major-subunit materials are underestimated in 1954, since only 1963 data were used to estimate the necessary parameters. In fact, the exact correspondence between the predicted and actual amounts of Rules 7C and 7E in 1963 takes place for the same reason. Finally, with respect to nonrecurring revenues the large divergence in 1954 is due to the aftereffects of errors in Rules 7A through 7E.

Explanation of Chart 5

A detailed account of the process for removing deficits (*SEARCH*) appears in Chart 5. It is activated if $\Delta 1$, the prediction of the surplus for $t+1$, is negative. The first step in the process is to determine whether the preliminary value of the provision for unexpended appropriations (*PROV*) is below its allowable limit. If not, this course of action must be bypassed. Otherwise, assuming that the magnitude of the deficit ($|\Delta 1|$) is less than or equal to the allowable increase in the provision, miscellaneous expenditures (*MISC-EXP*), which contains the provision, is decreased by $|\Delta 1|$. Accordingly, the budget is balanced and the program halts. However, if $|\Delta 1|$ is greater than the allowable increase in the provision, *MISCEXP* and $|\Delta 1|$ are reduced by the allowable increase.

Next the model inquires about the expectations of added funds for $t+2$ (*EXP 2*). If expectations are favorable (*EXP* 2 = 1), then the remaining deficit is removed by an increase in the revenue forecasts (*BALANCE*). If expectations are unfavorable (*EXP* 2 = 0), reductions of the expenditure side of the budget continue.

Suppose that the magnitude of the remaining deficit is less than the preliminary appropriation for account 30140 (*BLDGALT*). Then the model's prediction of the school buildings appropriation (E_1), which contains account 30140, is decreased by the deficit; the budget is balanced and the program halts. If the magnitude of $\Delta 1$ is larger than *BLDGALT*, E_1 and the deficit are decreased by *BLDGALT* and the process moves to the next level.

Here the maximum allowable cut in fringe services is .07 times their total preliminary personnel allocation (*FREXP*). If the amount of the remaining deficit is the same or smaller, fixed obligations (*FINLAW*), which contains *FREXP*, is reduced by $|\Delta 1|$ and the program halts. If not, then *FINLAW* and the deficit are reduced by the allowable cut and the routine goes to the next level.

Now reductions in the preliminary new-personnel appropriations of the major subunits (the PE_i) are considered. The allowable limit for cuts is the total preliminary new-personnel outlay (*PE*) minus either the preliminary committee-work allocation for $t+1$ (PE_1) or the preliminary committee-work allocation for t (PY_1), whichever is smaller. In other words, it is assumed that committee work will not be cut below the smaller of PE_1 or PY_1. If $|\Delta 1|$ is less than or equal to the allowable limit, the portion of committee work eligible for reduction and all other new-personnel accounts are reduced by a fraction (F_{NP}), whose value insures that the deficit will be eliminated. If the amount of the deficit is larger than the allowable limit, the committee-work outlay is set equal to PE_1 or PY_1, whichever is smaller, and all other new-personnel appropriations are eliminated. In addition, $|\Delta 1|$ is reduced by the total cut from this level.

Next, reductions are made in the preliminary materials appropriations of the major subunits (the E_i). The maximum allowable reduction is .05 times the total preliminary materials allocation (L) If the remaining deficit is the same or smaller than this amount, each materials account is reduced by a fraction (F_M), the value of which insures that the deficit will be eliminated. If the remaining deficit is larger, all materials accounts are reduced by 5 percent and $|\Delta 1|$ is trimmed accordingly.

Finally, if a deficit remains at this point, methods that affect the revenue side of the budget will be utilized. The budget will be balanced and the program will halt.

Excess-Distribution Processes

When forecasted revenues exceed preliminary expenditures, a set of decisions must be made to distribute the surplus. An overview of the process is presented in Chart 1. First, it is necessary to determine how much should be allocated as recurring (RS) and nonrecurring spending (NRS). Suppose that the year for which the budget is being prepared is even (the legislature met this year). Then it will be at least two years until a sizeable amount of additional funds can be expected. Hence, any recurring spending scheduled for the next year ($t+1$) will have to be sustained in the year after the next also ($t+2$). In order to discover the limit on recurring spending for $t+1$ the following procedure is used: A projection of the surplus in $t+2$ is made, taking into consideration only those decisions for $t+1$ that have been made up to this point ($\Delta 2$). The pertinent revenue figure in the calculation is the school system's forecast of revenues for $t+2$ minus net added spending to originate in that year ($NETREV\ 2$). This figure is supplied to the model.

Now let us look at the expenditure side of the calculation. The school system assumes that its spending already decided upon for $t+1$ will be carried over to $t+2$ at the same levels.[2] This assump-

[2] The only exception is $NEWDEBT$, which must be increased under certain conditions. If working capital is between $-2,500,000 and $-3,500,-

tion was adopted in the model, but applied to the expenditure pre dictions for $t+1$. As a result, the model's prediction of $\Delta 2$ differs from the school system's.[3]

Now suppose $\Delta 2$ is greater than or equal to zero. If $\Delta 1$ (which cannot be negative) is less than or equal to $\Delta 2$, recurring spending equal to $\Delta 1$ is planned for the coming year. This process (*SLACK*) will assign new personnel to the major subunits and may result in new fringe benefits. If $\Delta 1$ is larger than $\Delta 2$, recurring spending equal to $\Delta 2$ is distributed to the same budget categories. In addition, nonrecurring spending equal to $\Delta 1$ minus $\Delta 2$ will be distributed to the major departments for materials.

Assuming $\Delta 2$ is negative, $\Delta 1$ will be distributed as nonrecurring spending. This means that a special-contingency category will be established to handle particular problems anticipated to occur in $t+1$, and any remaining funds will be distributed to the major subunits for materials.

The final path to be explored occurs when it is found that $\Delta 1 \geq 0$, but the budget year is odd (the state legislature meets the next year). It is expected that the legislature will provide enough funds for $t+2$ so that the surplus appropriations for $t+1$ may be continued. In this situation, recurring expenditures equal in magnitude to $\Delta 1$ are distributed for new personnel and perhaps fringe benefits.

In order to complete discussion of the model the content of the processes which distribute recurring and nonrecurring funds will be explained in detail. An important use of recurring funds is to

---

000, then only one semiannual interest payment need be appropriated for the next year. However, by the year after, this obligation will grow to one principal payment and two semiannual interest payments.

[3] If added funds are not expected from the next session of the state legislature, a four-year planning period is required. Recurring spending for the next year must be sustained for three years afterwards. The pertinent value of $\Delta 2$ comes from the year with the smallest surplus. In order to build this exceptional case into the model the length of the planning period is actually taken as given rather than as being two years.

ovide fringe benefits for the employees of the school system. The growing significance of fringe benefits as a means of compensation has already been noted in related literature. The general conclusion seems to be that they are steadily increasing their share of the total wage bundle.[4] Unfortunately, the reasons for this phenomenon are not yet clearly understood, although some speculation has occurred. In discussing the motivation of employers, both economic and political implications seem to have emerged. On the economic side, Allan M. Cartter and F. Ray Marshall suggest that increases in fringe benefits cost less than an equivalent wage increase, because when the latter occurs, social security, overtime, and other items must be affected.[5] On the "political" side, Richard A. Lester has contended that employers use benefits as a strategy for binding workers to the firm—at least to the extent that they are lost upon separation.[6] My own observations bear some relation to Lester's findings, but also introduce new considerations.

In the years between salary increases the dissatisfaction of teachers in the model's system with their compensation should be building up in intensity. There are at least two reasons why this dissatisfaction should result in pressure for fringe benefits instead of small salary increases. We are talking, first of all, about years in which the teachers' salary schedule has not yet fallen to its critical level. Hence, it is likely that other aspects of the wage bundle will generate more concern. Second, new benefits have the advantage of imposing an added responsibility upon the employer, which in

[4] For example, Melvin Lurie, using Department of Commerce data, has indicated in "The Growth of Fringe Benefits and the Meaning of Wage Setting by Wage Comparisons," *The Journal of Industrial Economics,* 15, no. 1 (November, 1966): 19, that wage and salary supplements were 1.1% of total wages and salaries in 1929, but grew to 11.6% of the total by 1962.

[5] Allan M. Cartter and F. Ray Marshall, *Labor Economics: Wages, Employment, and Trade Unionism* (Homewood, Ill.: Richard D. Irwin, 1967), p. 338.

[6] Richard A. Lester, *Economics of Labor,* 2d ed. (New York: Macmillan, 1964), p. 260.

time can also be increased.[7] Now suppose that the administration finds itself with surplus recurring funds at a time when the dissatisfaction of teachers is beginning to mount. An affirmative reply toward a request for fringe benefits would be expected because benefits represent a relatively inexpensive way of maintaining harmonious personnel relations. Once more, all employees should share in receiving them because of the organizational norm for equitable treatment.

In order to test these theories an attempt was made to compile a history of fringe-benefit allocations from the 1954 to 1965 budgets. Unfortunately, it was not possible to gather reliable data on increases in existing benefits, so concentration was focused on the study of new ones. A list of those new benefits granted on the district's initiative instead of in compliance with legal regulations

Table 17—New Fringe Benefits

Budget	Item	Amount	RS^a	CD^b
1955	Group insurance	$ 85,000	$254,000	2
1959	—	0	−728,000	1
1961	Major medical insurance	25,600	196,000	4
1965	Personal leave	100,000	527,000	4
	Hospitalization	235,000		

[a]Surplus recurring funds.

[b]CD = number of comparable districts with lower B.A. starting salaries in autumn of previous year.

appears in Table 17. They include group insurance initiated in the 1955 budget, major medical insurance in the 1961 budget, and hospitalization and personal leave in the 1965 budget. Such improvements in working conditions as lower teaching loads have been ignored because there is no practical way of determining their history.

[7] See Arthur M. Ross, "The External Wage Structure," in *New Concepts in Wage Determination,* ed. George W. Taylor and Frank C. Pierson (New York: McGraw-Hill, 1957), p. 183.

The fringe benefits of Table 17 should have been inaugurated in years for which surplus recurring funds were expected and the dissatisfaction of teachers was building up. To measure the teachers' dissatisfaction, the salary index—the number of comparable districts with lower B.A. starting salaries (CD)—was used. It has been shown that when CD has a value of 0 there is enough dissatisfaction confronting the administration to bring forth a salary increase. Hence, a value anywhere from 1 to D, where D is much smaller than the maximum of 17, would indicate mounting dissatisfaction.

An analysis of the data revealed that new fringe benefits have been granted when and only when recurring surplus funds, as the term has been defined, were available, and the salary index's value was between 1 and 4. In addition, it appears that all employees shared in receiving them. A compilation of the evidence for the first point appears in Table 17. Those budgets for which the value of CD was 0 or greater than 4 were not included, since no new benefits appeared in them. It may be concluded that as the value of the salary index falls, new benefits are granted first (provided it is financially reasonable), and then salary increases. This observation agrees with other research which has shown that as employee dissatisfaction goes up, a preference appears for more wages as opposed to benefits.[8]

The amount of new benefits which will be granted was estimated by referring to the three pertinent budgets in Table 17. The fraction of recurring surplus funds allocated for this use was 0.34 in 1955, 0.13 in 1961, and 0.64 in 1965. It is unlikely that these widely divergent values came from the same distribution because of the changes that occurred over the eleven-year timespan. Therefore, the most recent value was used as the estimate. It is now possible to state the model's decision rule for this part of the process:

> *Rule 8:* If $RS > 0$ and $1 \leq CD \leq 4$, then provide new fringe benefits in an amount equal to 0.64 RS.

[8] See Stanley M. Nealey, "Pay and Benefit Preference," *Industrial Relations,* 3, no. 1 (October, 1963): 27.

The development of that portion of the theory which distributes recurring and nonrecurring funds to the major subunits was severely handicapped by the depth to which analysis could reach. There have only been three budgets from 1954 to 1965 (1960, 1962, 1965) in which sizeable amounts of funds were distributed to the major subunits. More important, little information could be obtained concerning the decisions on the first two of these occasions because no current staff member participated in making them. As a result, this part of the model is in general more descriptive than other aspects.

Recurring spending is divided in the following manner among the new-personnel accounts: First it is allocated among the three priorities so that the first receives more than the second, which in turn receives more than the third. Then, within the top priority, teachers receive the largest share and the balance is divided equally among the other accounts. In the other priorities the funds are divided equally.

Nonrecurring spending is allocated to materials accounts in a similar manner. It is first divided among the priority levels, taking into consideration their relative positions. Then, within the top level, texts receives the largest share and the balance is divided among the other accounts in proportion to their preliminary appropriations. In the second and third levels a proportional division is used for all accounts.

This process requires the estimation of six independent parameters, including the proportion of recurring spending allocated to the first priority (0.85), the proportion of recurring spending allocated to the second priority (0.15), the proportion of recurring spending within the first priority allocated for teachers (0.50), the proportion of nonrecurring spending allocated to the first priority (0.40), the proportion of nonrecurring spending allocated to the second priority (0.40), and the proportion of nonrecurring spending within the first priority allocated for texts (0.90). The data for parameter estimation come from the three budgets in which sizeable surpluses were available for distribution to the major subunits. The parame-

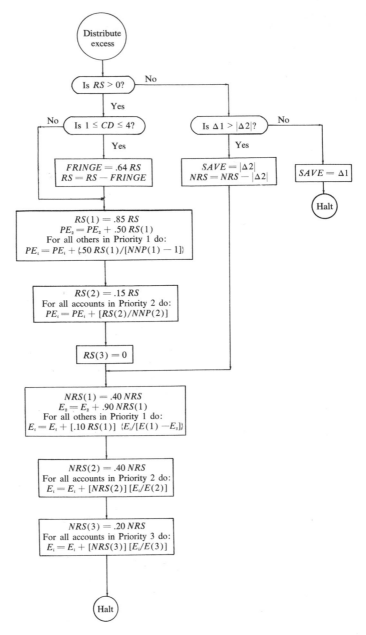

Chart 6. *SLACK*

ter values were determined using ratio estimates; the first one in the list above, for example, was the total recurring spending allocated to the first priority in these years, divided by the total recurring spending distributed to the major subunits in the same years.

A surplus, when it exists, is used partially as a device for keeping certain pressures from building up. It may be employed to maintain the morale of teachers by providing new fringe benefits in years between those in which salary increases are granted. Or it may be used to establish a special-contingency fund. Any remaining funds will be allocated to the major subunits, with teachers and texts receiving the largest shares.

Explanation of Chart 6

A detailed flow diagram of the process by which excess funds are allocated is presented in Chart 6. First an inquiry is made to see whether allowable recurring spending (RS) is greater than 0. If not, then a deficit had to have been projected for $t+2$. In this case the special contingency ($SAVE$) enters the budget and nonrecurring spending (NRS) is reduced by this amount.

When allowable recurring spending is greater than 0, the number of comparable districts whose B.A. minimum salary is less than the model's (CD) is determined. If CD has a value from 1 to 4, then new fringe benefits ($FRINGE$) are provided for all employees. Accordingly, allowable recurring spending is reduced by this amount. Any remaining recurring funds are distributed as additions to the new-personnel appropriations of the major subunits (the PE_i). The first priority's share [$RS(1)$] is 85 percent of the total. One half is added to the allocation for new teachers (PE_2) and the other half is divided equally among the priority's other new-personnel accounts. Here, $NNP(1)$ is the number of accounts in the first priority. The second priority's amount [$RS(2)$] is the remaining 15 percent, which is divided equally among its accounts, the number of which is $NNP(2)$. The third priority's share [$RS(3)$] is, of course, zero.

Next, any remaining nonrecurring funds are allocated as additions to the materials appropriations of the major subunits (the E_i). The first priority's amount [$NRS(1)$] is 40 percent of the total. Nine-tenths is added to the textbook allocation (E_2) and the rest is divided among the priority's other materials accounts in proportion to their preliminary appropriations. Here, $E(1)$ represents the total preliminary materials appropriation for the first priority. The shares of the second and third groups [$NRS(2)$ and $NRS(3)$] are divided among their accounts in proportion to preliminary appropriations. Here, $E(2)$ and $E(3)$ represent the total preliminary materials allocation to each priority. The budget is now balanced and the program halts.

6

Tests and Sensitivity Analysis

Now that the model has been presented, it is time to discover how well it conforms to reality by testing its predictions against actual decisions. In doing so, the main emphasis will be placed on materials because that category accounts for the majority of appropriations. In addition, sensitivity analyses will be performed in order to estimate the extent to which certain parameters of the model are influential and to provide an example of how the model may be used as a planning tool by public administrators.

Testing the Model

The current state of knowledge concerning the testing of simulation models must be regarded as inadequate at best. The situation has been summed up by Thomas H. Naylor and J. M. Finger with the following comments: ". . . management scientists have had very little to say about how one goes about 'verifying' a simulation model or the data generated by such a model on a digital computer. In part, the reason for avoiding the subject of verification stems from the fact that the problem of verifying or validating computer models remains today perhaps the most elusive of all the unresolved methodological problems associated with computer simulation techniques."[1] Fortunately, Naylor and Finger have also

[1] Thomas H. Naylor and J. M. Finger, "Verification of Computer Simulation Models," *Management Science,* 14, no. 2 (October, 1967): 92.

been able to suggest a useful framework within which tests may be conducted. It involves a "multi-stage" verification procedure with three components:[2] (1) testing of the model's assumptions on a priori grounds, such as their conformity to existing theory; (2) empirical testing of the model's assumptions; and (3) empirical testing of the closeness of fit between the model's outputs and the observed data.

One reason for the usefulness of Naylor and Finger's framework is that it highlights the importance of examining assumptions as well as predictions. To some extent my assumptions have been compared to existing theory (as, for example, in the discussion of compensation decisions); more extensive comparisons of this type will be made in Chapter 8. It has also been my aim, wherever possible, to test empirically the assumptions behind any decision rules which have been discovered. The statistical testing of the expectations and priority effects done in Chapter 3 is a case in point.

The final stage, the testing of the fit between the model's outputs and the observed data, will be taken up in this chapter. Kalman J. Cohen and Richard M. Cyert have pointed out that the most difficult problems in step 3 arise when the model's outputs are time-series data. "Testing the conformity of generated time series to actual data is a problem because of the many possible dimensions which could meaningfully be used. . . . At present there is no single test which will consider all the relevant time-series dimensions at once. The only recourse is to use individual tests for particular properties. This means, in fact, that a great deal of judgment must enter into the evaluation of computer models."[3]

In this case it is possible to bypass some of these problems because the model in its present form does not generate time-series data. It should be classified as a "one-period-change model," since it makes predictions for just one year ahead, provided values are assigned to the exogenous variables. Hence, standard statistical

[2] *Ibid.*, p. 95.
[3] Kalman J. Cohen and Richard M. Cyert, "Simulation of Organizational Behavior," in *Handbook of Organizations,* ed. James G. March (Chicago: Rand McNally, 1965), p. 331.

techniques may be used to compare the model's predictions to actual decisions.[4] Before discussing the statistical tests that were employed, it must be pointed out that they were conducted on the same budgets (1961–1965) used to estimate parameters.

The most important set of outputs to test are the final materials allocations to the major subunits, since these account for the majority of predicted appropriations. Preliminary materials decisions also require testing to help determine whether the process that leads to the final decisions has been accurately described. It must be pointed out that over the testing period, preliminary and final materials predictions differed in only one year. This occurred when a deficit had to be eliminated, which implies that the portion of the model that distributes excess nonrecurring funds to the major subunits was not utilized.

In the first set of tests, regression analysis was used to compare actual allocations (dependent variable) to predicted appropriations (independent variable). This technique provides an examination of at least three important characteristics: A constant bias in predictions can be found, for example, by examining whether the constant term (a) is significantly different from 0 ($H_0 : a = 0$ vs. $H_1 : a \neq 0$).[5] It can also be determined whether a multiplicative bias exists by testing to see if the slope (β) is significantly different from 1 ($H_0 : \beta = 1$ vs. $H_1 : \beta \neq 1$). Finally, even if there is no reason to believe that there are biases of this sort in the predictions, the points may still be widely scattered about the estimated regression line. This condition, which indicates that the predictions are subject to a great deal of random error, may be examined by estimating the correlation coefficient (ρ). The results are presented in Table 18, where confidence intervals are calculated on all three parameters. Here, there are 115 sample points representing the twenty-three major subunits in each of five years. There is no evidence at the .05 level that preliminary or final predictions

[4] *Ibid.*
[5] As in standard statistical terminology, H_0 represents the hypothesis to be tested and H_1 represents the alternative hypothesis.

Table 18—Regression Analysis for Materials Predictions

H_0	Estimated value	95% confidence interval	Accept H_0
	Preliminary predictions		
$\alpha = 0$	-136	$-2{,}735 < \alpha < 2{,}463$	Yes
$\beta = 1$	.978	$.966 < \beta < .990$	No
Correlation coefficient (ρ)	.998	$.997 < \rho < .998$	—
	Final predictions		
$\alpha = 0$	7,280	$-1{,}352 < \alpha < 15{,}912$	Yes
$\beta = 1$	.903	$.861 < \beta < .946$	No
Correlation coefficient (ρ)	.969	$.955 < \rho < .975$	—

have a constant bias, since the pertinent intervals include 0. There is reason to believe that both sets of predictions have a multiplicative bias because the intervals do not include 1. The bias appears, however, to be negligible for preliminary decisions and not large for the final ones. The confidence intervals on the correlation coefficient suggest that that parameter has a high value in both cases, which further implies that the predictions are subject to little random error.

The next set of tests involved a comparison of the model's materials predictions to five naive forecasting methods'. Preliminary appropriations were predicted using:

1. $R_{i,t+1}$ (request of ith major subunit for $t+1$).
2. $Y_{i,t}$ (preliminary appropriation to i^{th} major subunit for t).
3. $\dfrac{Y_{i,t}}{Y_t}$ (Y_{t+1}), where Y_t = total preliminary materials allocation to the major subunits for t (each major subunit receives the same fraction it preliminarily received for t).
4. $A_{i,t}$ (final appropriation to i^{th} major subunit for t)
5. $\dfrac{A_{i,t}}{A_t}(Y_{t+1})$, where A_t = total final materials allocation to

the major subunits for t (each major subunit receives the same fraction it finally received for t).

The same five methods are used to predict final materials appropriations except that in methods 3 and 5, Y_{t+1} is replaced by A_{t+1}.

The model was evaluated against the naive methods by comparing the absolute percentage errors of its individual major-subunit predictions with the absolute percentage errors of their predictions. A compilation appears in Table 19, where the number of sample

Table 19—Comparison of Absolute Percentage Errors

Method	0–5%	5+–25%	25+–50%	>50%
	Preliminary decisions			
Model	76	28	4	5
Naive 1	76	16	11	10
Naive 2	53	34	11	15
Naive 3	13	76	10	14
Naive 4	36	38	13	26
Naive 5	14	48	24	27
	Final decisions			
Model	65	30	9	9
Naive 1	60	22	15	16
Naive 2	40	40	14	19
Naive 3	11	63	21	18
Naive 4	24	44	18	27
Naive 5	13	45	28	27

points is 113 since 2 preliminary and 2 final points had actual allocations of zero. In each cell appears the number of predictions of a particular method whose errors were in the indicated range. An examination of the table reveals that the model does at least as well as any of the naive methods. For example, whether preliminary or final decisions are considered, the model has at least as many predictions in the 0 percent to 5 percent group as any other method, and less predictions in the > 50 percent group. In addition, whether preliminary or final decisions are considered, there are more model predictions in the 0 percent to 25 percent group and fewer in the > 25 percent group than any other method. In order to find statistical verification for these intuitive notions, contingency tables were formed from the data in Table 19. The four rows of each table are the percentage error ranges, 0–5 percent, 5^+–25 percent, 25^+–50 percent and > 50 percent, while the two columns represent the model's percentage errors and a particular naive method's. A test of homogeneity was employed to see whether any differences existed between the two error distributions in each

Table 20—Overall Errors of Materials Predictions

Model	Preliminary decisions	Final decisions
Model	4.7%	12.9%
Naive 1	7.5	20.3
Naive 2	16.2	26.2
Naive 3	18.4	27.5
Naive 4	32.2	36.9
Naive 5	34.0	37.2

table.[6] On this basis the first naive method $(R_{i,t+1})$ proved to be equal to the model as far as final decisions are concerned. In all other cases the model did better than the naive methods at the .05 level.

An overall measure of comparability between the model's materials predictions and the naive forecasts was also constructed. The absolute errors of a given method's individual predictions over the entire test period were added, then multiplied by 100 and divided by the total actual allocation to the major subunits over the five years. This was done separately for preliminary and final decisions. Table 20 reveals that in both instances the model performs better than any naive method.

[6] See Wilfrid J. Dixon and Frank J. Massey, *Introduction to Statistical Analysis,* 2d ed. (New York: McGraw-Hill, 1957), p. 225.

Table 21—Errors of Total New-Personnel Predictions

	Preliminary decisions			
Budget	Actual allocation	Model	Requests	Current preliminary allocation
1961	$ 37,300	0.0%	318.0%	−100.0%
1962	70,000	−34.0	133.0	−47.0
1963	52,000	0.0	432.0	35.0
1964	203,640	−1.0	80.0	−75.0
1965	561,033	−10.0	28.0	−64.0
Overall	$923,973	9.0%	81.0%	65.0%

	Final decisions			
Budget	Actual allocation	Model	Requests	Current final allocation
1961	$ 37,295	23.0%	318.0%	425.0%
1962	265,772	66.0	−39.0	−86.0
1963	27,528	45.0	905.0	865.0
1964	233,640	−13.0	56.0	−88.0
1965	643,983	11.0	11.0	−64.0
Overall	$1,208,218	25.0%	56.0%	103.0%

In discussing tests on new-personnel appropriations for the major subunits it should be remembered that this is not a large component of the budget. For the years 1961 to 1965 their ratio to major-subunit materials appropriations was 0.02, 0.12, 0.02, 0.09, and 0.20, respectively. Hence, tests were not conducted on an individual account basis as was done for materials.

First let us examine how successful the model was in predicting the total amount of funds allocated for new personnel. In order to make comparisons, preliminary appropriations also are forecast, using the total amount of requests and the total amount of current preliminary allocations. In dealing with final appropriations requests and current final allocations were used. The yearly predictions of each method were gauged using the percentage error:

$$\frac{100 \times (\text{total predicted amount for the year} - \text{total actual amount for the year})}{\text{total actual amount for the year}}$$

A method's overall worth was calculated by summing the absolute values of the yearly numerators and dividing by the sum of the yearly denominators. Referring to Table 21, it appears that all the model's preliminary predictions are better than those of the other methods. Also, while the error for 1962 is high, the magnitude involved is small. The results for final predictions show the model to do at least as well in all years except 1962. It has high errors especially for 1961, 1962, and 1963, but the magnitudes involved for 1961 and 1963 are small.

Unfortunately, there is one respect in which the results of Table 21 present a somewhat distorted picture. The main reason for the poor performance of the method based on requests is that a single department, special education, continually asked for unusually large amounts of funds. If the errors of this method and the model are recalculated disregarding special education, the model does not fare as well as previously. For example, the overall preliminary error of the model drops to 7 percent but that of the naive method drops to 15 percent. Considering final decisions the naive method's overall error is 27 percent as compared to the model's 33 percent.

These tests serve to indicate that the model's total final allocations could have been more accurate, especially for 1962. Not as much of the available surplus recurring funds as would be expected went to the major-subunit new-personnel accounts in that budget.

Another set of tests considered not only the model's *total* new-personnel decisions, but also its allocation of funds. Here, the same naive methods as used before were employed. A yearly error measure was obtained by adding the absolute errors of a given method's individual major-subunit predictions in any year, multiplying by 100, and dividing by the total actual allocation in that year. An overall measure was calculated in the same manner except that the numerator and denominator were based on the entire five-year

Table 22—Absolute Errors of New-Personnel Predictions

		Preliminary decisions		
Budget	Actual allocation	Model	Requests	Current preliminary allocation
1961	$ 37,300	0.0%	317.7%	100.0%
1962	70,000	51.4	219.1	46.7
1963	52,000	0.0	431.9	80.8
1964	203,640	7.8	88.5	74.5
1965	561,033	10.4	29.4	63.7
Overall	$923,973	12.0%	91.0%	67.2%

		Final decisions		
Budget	Actual allocation	Model	Requests	Current final allocation
1961	$ 37,295	22.4%	317.7%	446.4%
1962	265,772	129.2	73.7	86.0
1963	27,528	378.2	1094.5	865.2
1964	233,640	19.6	89.7	95.4
1965	643,983	25.6	38.5	63.7
Overall	$1,208,218	55.2%	88.8%	104.8%

period; the overall measure is therefore the same as that used in the tests of materials predictions. The results appear in Table 22 and in general are similar to those of the tests just discussed. In the case of preliminary decisions the model does better overall and in all years except 1962, but in that year the magnitude of the error is small. For final decisions the model has high errors, but relatively speaking they are low except in 1962. If special education is eliminated and only the model and the naive method based on requests are considered, the advantage of the model diminishes. On a preliminary basis the model's overall error is 10 percent as compared to the naive method's 20 percent, but considering final decisions the model is outperformed 43 percent to 53 percent. The most serious problem revealed by this set of tests is the model's difficulty in accurately allocating surplus recurring funds to the major subunits, especially for 1962. However, as explained previously, it was not possible to refine the findings on this aspect of the process.

A final method of analysis is employed to help answer the question of whether the process by which other decisions are made has been accurately predicted. The decisions tested are salary increases, new debt service other than interest on temporary loans, the distribution of surplus funds versus the deficit-removal process (mutually exclusive in the model but not necessarily in the actual situation), new fringe benefits, and the special-contingency fund.

In Table 23 the occurrence of a decision is represented by a 1 and the nonoccurrence by a 0. The surplus-distribution process is designated by 1, while the deficit-removal process is assigned a 0 value. The amount of funds associated with each choice is indicated in italics. In every instance the model has correctly determined whether or not the *SALINC, NEWDEBT, FRINGE,* and *SAVE* decisions would be made. For *SEARCH/SLACK* the model is hampered by its inability to simultaneously distribute funds and cut spending. In the 1962 budget, spending was cut $663,000 in order to enlarge an already existing surplus to a new total of $938,046, which accounts for the two extra numbers in the pertinent cell of Table 23. The model, however, was only able to predict that a surplus would be distributed. Also, in the 1961 and 1964 budgets relatively small cuts were made in spending even though surpluses were forecast. These are not indicated in Table 23 as examples of the *SEARCH* process because they appeared to be due to improved estimations of preliminary spending rather than to intentional attempts to use the deficit-removal process for the purpose of enlarging the surplus. Finally, in the 1963 budget a relatively small amount of appropriations was added after it was known that a deficit was in the making. This is not considered as an occurrence of the *SLACK* process because it seemed to result from efforts to handle some problems peculiar to that year.

The model's inability to take note of simultaneous additions and subtractions in appropriations is an important reason for the dis-

Table 23—Other Decisions[a]

Decision	1961 Actual	1961 Model	1962 Actual	1962 Model	1963 Actual	1963 Model	1964 Actual	1964 Model	1965 Actual	1965 Model
SALINC	0	0	1 *1,696,790*	1 *1,690,650*	0	0	1 *520,715*	1 *450,261*	0	0
NEWDEBT	0	0	1 *87,500*	1 *87,500*	0	0	1 *356,250*	1 *375,000*	0	0
SEARCH/SLACK	1 *195,624*	1 *23,255*	0 *663,000* / 1 *938,046*	1 *395,887*	0 *1,468,355*	0 *1,291,315*	1 *1,348,000*	1 *1,276,399*	1 *526,950*	1 *583,794*
FRINGE	1 *25,600*	1 *14,883*	0	0	0	0	0	0	1 *335,000*	1 *373,678*
SAVE	0	0	0	0	0	0	1 *1,040,600*	1 *1,276,399*	0	0

[a]The occurrence of the deficit-removal process (*SEARCH*) is represented by a 0 and the surplus-distribution process (*SLACK*) by a 1. Numbers in italics are in terms of dollars.

crepancies between actual and predicted amounts in the 1961 through 1965 columns of the *SEARCH/SLACK* row. The actual and predicted amounts of the other decisions in Table 23 all compare more or less favorably. Some of the favorable correspondence, however, must be attributed to the fact that certain predictions are based on the actual amounts to which they are being compared. The primary examples are *SALINC* in 1962 and *FRINGE* in 1965. The model seems to have done a better job in predicting when the decisions of Table 23 are made than how much will be appropriated.

Sensitivity Analysis

For reasons which have been explained previously some parameters in the model have been estimated without a great deal of data. Since these estimates are likely to be imprecise, it is important to discover whether they greatly influence the model's output. A sensitivity analysis is perhaps the best way to examine the degree of change in the model's predictions caused by varying these parameters. Suppose a parameter estimated from sparse data is allowed to range through a wide continuum of possible values. If predictions are hardly affected, it may be concluded that the lack of precision is not very costly.

The specific set of outputs which will gauge the importance of the parameters are the final materials allocations to the major subunits, since they account for a majority of appropriations. The effect on individual materials allocations caused by a change in a parameter was measured by calculating the mean and standard deviation of the sample consisting of the ratio

$$\frac{E'_{i,t+1}}{E_{i,t+1}} \qquad \begin{aligned} i &= 1, 2, \ldots, 23 \\ t+1 &= 1961, 1962, \ldots, 1965 \end{aligned}$$

where

$E'_{i,t+1}$ = final materials prediction for the ith major subunit in year $t+1$ when a given change is made in the value of the parameter being studied, and

$E_{i, t+1}$ = final materials prediction for the ith major subunit in year $t+1$ when no parameters are changed.

A ratio is used in order to lessen statistical dependence among the predictions for the same subunit in different years. The effect on aggregate materials predictions is measured by calculating

$$\frac{\Sigma_{i, t} \, E'_{i, t+1}}{\Sigma_{i, t} \, E_{i, t+1}}.$$

In order to establish standards of comparison define $E'_{i, t+1} = E_{i, t+1}$ when the parameter being studied takes on its estimated value. Then the mean and standard deviation of the sample ratios are 1 and 0 respectively and the value of the aggregate measure is 1.

The parameters which affect preliminary predictions for subunits of the third priority in high years (P_{31}), second priority in low years (P_{22}), and third priority in low years (P_{32}) were examined first. Each of the estimated values was increased and decreased by 25 percent. The results as compiled in Table 24 indicate that such changes have little effect on predictions. For example, a 25 percent change in P_{22} causes the ratio's mean to vary by only about 3 percent.

The parameters of the deficit-removal process were also investigated, including the upper limits on the provision for unexpended appropriations (P_1), on the fraction of the fringe-activities appropriations that can be cut (P_2), and on the fraction of the major-subunit materials appropriations that can be removed (P_3). Since the model utilizes the deficit-removal process in only one year, there is not a sufficient basis for measuring the influence of these parameters on final materials predictions. In order to have the model utilize the process more frequently, it was necessary in each year to increase fixed obligations $(FINLAW)$ by 2 percent and to rule out the availability of the revenue-reinvestigation method by setting $EXP\ 2 = 0$. This action required a redefinition of the sensitivity measures to eliminate the effects of the changes in $FINLAW$

Table 24—Changes in Individual Parameters

Parameter	Parameter value	Mean	Standard deviation	Aggregate measure
P_{31}	0.84	0.991	0.064	0.992
	1.12	1.000	0.000	1.000
	1.40	1.010	0.044	1.007
P_{22}	0.81	0.965	0.087	0.984
	1.08	1.000	0.000	1.000
	1.35	1.030	0.079	1.011
P_{32}	0.75	0.980	0.068	0.984
	1.00	1.000	0.000	1.000
	1.25	1.012	0.045	1.010
P_1	200,000	0.998	0.012	0.949
	405,000	1.000	0.000	1.000
	600,000	1.004	0.040	0.980
P_2	0.00	1.000	0.000	1.000
	0.07	1.000	0.000	1.000
	0.35	1.000	0.000	1.000
P_3	0.00	1.011	0.021	0.973
	0.05	1.000	0.000	1.000
	0.25	0.957	0.085	0.931
F_T	0.68	1.002	0.021	—
	0.90	1.000	0.000	—
	1.00	0.999	0.009	—

and $EXP\,2$ on final materials predictions. In particular, $E'_{i,t+1}$ and $E_{i,\,t+1}$ were calculated, using the new values of $FINLAW$ and $EXP\,2$ rather than the estimated ones. Table 24 reveals that materials predictions were insensitive to the induced changes in the three parameters of the deficit-removal process. The largest change in the ratio's mean (about 4 percent) was produced by a five-fold increase in P_3.

The parameters which determine the distribution of surplus nonrecurring funds to the major subunits were tested next. Since this part of the model was not utilized for the years 1961–1965, any change in its parameters cannot affect final materials predictions.

Consequently, it was necessary to reduce $FINLAW$ by 2 percent in order to generate a nonrecurring surplus in some years. The sensitivity measures were changed in the same way as they had been for the deficit-removal process. The parameters investigated were the fraction of appropriations for the first priority awarded to texts (F_T) and the fraction of nonrecurring funds allocated to the jth priority (F_j, where $j = 1, 2, 3$). Since changes in these parameters may influence the distribution of appropriations to particular accounts but not the total amount of funds available, the aggregate measure is of no value here. F_T was reduced 25 percent and also raised to its upper limit of 1.00, but Table 24 reveals virtually no effect on predictions. The three F_j values were changed simultaneously because they are not independent. In Table 25 the first row

Table 25 Changes in Surplus-Distribution Parameters

F_1	F_2	F_3	Mean	Standard deviation
0.80	0.20	0.00	0.963	0.128
0.40	0.40	0.20	1.000	0.000
0.33	0.33	0.33	1.003	0.068
0.00	0.20	0.80	1.029	0.297

represents a stronger priority effect than originally estimated, the second row shows the estimated values, the third row assumes no priority effect, and the last row assumes a relatively strong priority effect in the reverse direction. The results show that materials predictions are not greatly affected by these changes.

The Model as an Aid in Planning

Sensitivity analysis can also be used to show the effect on the budget of varying internal policies and external constraints. This means that the new allocation of expenditures can be determined; it does not mean that the associated change in benefits can be estimated. Therefore, the model is only a partial aid in the planning process.

For the sake of illustration consider the internal-policy parameter, which indicates the number of comparable districts whose minimum teachers' salary must be below the model's before a salary increase will be granted (P_S). The estimated value of P_S was 0. The impact on the 1961 to 1965 budgets of raising its value to 4 and then to 8 was tested. Increasing P_S implies that the district is aspiring to more of a position of salary-schedule leadership. When $P_S = 0$, there is only one occasion on which the system decides to grant a general salary increase; $1,691,000 is allocated for this purpose.[7] When $P_S = 4$, three increases are provided which cost $4,211,000. When $P_S = 8$, there are four raises totaling $5,027,000.

The areas of the budget which must be cut in order to maintain a balance can also be determined. The benefits accruing from these areas represent the price of changing the salary policy and must be weighed against the latter's benefits, such as attracting better-quality teachers. If the price appears to be too high, the possibility of alternative cuts may be explored by changing the rules in the deficit-elimination process.

The allocative implications of a change in a particular external constraint may be investigated by discussing the 2 percent adjustments in fixed obligations $(FINLAW)$ mentioned earlier in the chapter.[8] The upward change had virtually no effect on final materials decisions, using the ratio's average as a measure. However, the downward adjustment had a substantial effect: the measure increased by 14 percent. If this analysis had been performed as the result of an impending change in $FINLAW$, it would have provided advance information as to the probable effects on the budget. As an analysis of a hypothetical change it suggests that if possible some of the components of $FINLAW$ should be renegotiated.

There are innumerable other types of issues that could be explored. The effects on the budget of an alteration in the priority

---

[7] General salary increases motivated by the state's decision to raise teachers' wages are excluded from consideration since their effects are the same no matter what the value of P_S.

[8] The upward adjustment in $FINLAW$ was accompanied by setting $EXP\,2 = 0$.

system, an increase in the rate at which the comparable districts grant salary increases, or a change to an annual allocation of the state's educational funds could be examined. Moreover, various combinations of these adjustments could be tested and the model could be altered to perform its analysis for more than one year ahead.

Summary

It appears, therefore, that the model has adequately predicted materials appropriations, although a better job for preliminary as opposed to final decisions was done. The preliminary new-personnel predictions are satisfactory, but the final ones are not—mainly because a thorough understanding of the distribution of surplus recurring funds could not be obtained. The model has done very well in estimating the occurrences of certain other decisions, but not so well in determining their amounts. A sensitivity analysis revealed that none of the parameters investigated are likely to affect materials predictions in a substantial manner and illustrated the ability of the model to examine changes in policy and the environment.

7
An Analysis of
Budgetary Requests

An examination of Table 5 reveals that out of the 115 requests used as inputs to the model, 74 have been approved. In addition, Tables 19 and 20 indicate that the naive prediction method based on requests has the closest performance to that of the model. Since requests play an important role in the staff's decisions, it is necessary to provide some explanation of the process by which they are formulated.

Wildavsky's Theory

The following analysis will utilize a basic framework that has been developed by Aaron Wildavsky.[1] He has found that two general factors influence the magnitude of a federal agency's request: the base, that portion of the budget which is expected to be ongoing and which acts as a lower limit on the amount proposed; and environmental signals, which determine how much of an increase over this lower bound will be requested. Signals emanate from three main sources: the executive branch of the government, Congress, and the agency's public. The remarks of the President and the annual policy letter of the Bureau of the Budget, for example, are used to gauge the attitudes of the executive branch, while reports

[1] Aaron Wildavsky, *The Politics of the Budgetary Process* (Boston: Little, Brown and Co., 1964), pp. 21–31.

from the field, newspaper articles, and the visits of special-interest groups measure the feelings of the agency's clientele. Signals from Congress include its reaction to the specific proposals made by the agency in the previous year.

In order to apply Wildavsky's ideas to the model's school district, it is necessary to obtain an idea of where the environmental cues which impinge upon the directors of the major subunits originate. It is possible that the superintendent and his staff, the school board, the teachers and principals who use the items ordered by a subunit, the state government, various groups in the local community, and even the professional societies to which subunit directors belong will perform this function. It is also necessary to determine the nature of the pertinent environmental signals and to operationally define the base. Virtually all of the work done in the following sections is on materials because it was difficult to compile any meaningful results for new personnel. The primary sources of data for the investigation were the 1961 to 1965 budgets.

Consumables and Nonconsumables

There are two broad categories of materials requests which are not necessarily formulated in the same manner. Interviews and written justifications suggested that items which tend to be used up within a year or two are requested using different rules than are employed for items which tend to last for a number of years. The first group will be called consumables and the other nonconsumables. The consumable category is made up of the supplies accounts of the major subunits except for certain items which tend to last for a long period of time: textbooks; library supplies, which consist mainly of library books; films, which were previously included in audio-visual supplies; and social studies supplies, which consist of maps and globes.

The requests for consumables should contain a relatively large, stable component used for replacement purposes because it is necessary to constantly replenish these items. In addition, the current appropriation will represent, to a large extent, the result of all previous attempts to provide for this need. Therefore, it will have a relatively strong influence on the request. The nonconsumable component of a major subunit's materials request is the sum of repairs and replacements, capital outlay, and any supplies included in the list of exceptions above. Requests for nonconsumables will have a comparatively small erratic component used for replenishment. It will be small because capital outlay, which represents the purchase of new items, is not influenced by these considerations. It will be erratic because the need to repair and replace nonconsumables—a category composed of relatively few items, all of which tend to wear out—will change from one year to the next owing to their very nature. For these reasons, the current appropriation will have less of a relation to the request for the coming year than is true for consumables.

Evidence for this conclusion is supplied in Table 26, which shows

Table 26—Errors of Request Predictions Using Current Appropriations

Budget year ($t+1$)	Consumables		Nonconsumables	
	Preliminary appropriation for t	Final appropriation for t	Preliminary appropriation for t	Final appropriation for t
1961	10.8%	13.3%	22.9%	40.2%
1962	7.9	7.9	8.2	8.2
1963	11.6	6.5	29.0	24.6
1964	11.2	17.2	18.0	20.2
1965	13.4	13.4	26.8	26.8
Overall	11.1%	11.8%	21.8%	24.2%

the results of predicting major-subunit consumable and nonconsumable requests for $t+1$, using preliminary and final allocations for t. The numbers in the table represent yearly and overall percentage error measures computed in the same manner as in the previous chapter. The first is 100 times the sum of the absolute errors of a method's individual predictions for a given year, divided by the total amount actually requested for the year. The other is computed in the same manner except that the numerator and denominator are calculated over the entire test period. Clearly, the allocation for t, whether preliminary or final, performs better for consumables.[2]

Requests for Consumables

Over the five years from 1961 to 1965 consumable requests, as they have been defined, accounted for about 25 percent of the total amount of materials requests from the major subunits. In order to analyze their formulation they were classified into three groups; the purpose was to investigate whether different bases or environmental signals are used in each case. Upon letting $CY_i = i^{th}$ major subunit's preliminary appropriation for consumables for year t and $CA_i = i^{th}$ major subunit's final appropriation for consumables for t, we have (1) $CA_i = CY_i$, (2) $CA_i > CY_i$, and (3) $CA_i < CY_i$. The second situation occurs when the surplus-distribution process allocates funds to the major subunits, while the third case arises when the major subunits are affected by the deficit-removal process.

For fifty-seven out of the seventy-nine consumable requests examined, CA_i was found to equal CY_i.[3] Only one of the fifty-seven was found to be less in amount than appropriations for t. Therefore, it seems appropriate to use appropriations for t as the base in this situation. Although it could not be verified for every subunit in every year, increases in requests over the base appear to be influenced by a calculation of cost per pupil times number of pupils. By examining the environmental signals which affect these

[2] This suggests that the findings of Otto A. Davis, M. A. H. Dempster, and Aaron Wildavsky concerning the importance of the current allocation in request formulation should be qualified. It appears to have less of an influence on consumption goods than it does on investment goods. See "A Theory of the Budgetary Process," *American Political Science Review,* 60, no. 3 (September, 1966): 537.

[3] From this point on when I refer to requests, appropriations, and spending, I shall mean the consumable component.

two numbers it is possible to obtain an understanding of the forces which motivate increases. Of the factors which influence cost per pupil, the most frequently cited was price increases. In addition, new standards set by the state, and new ideas, which seem to originate with teachers or in professional society meetings, were also mentioned. The most important item affecting the number of pupils is enrollment increases in the particular area. These in turn may be due either to the expansion of a program or a net increase in the number of students entering the program.

Unfortunately, it was not possible to obtain measures of all these influences for every subunit in every year. Yet all of them eventually result in heightened signals from teachers and principals for additional appropriations. These signals can be measured by using requisitions—a method consistent with the frequent statements made by subunit directors that their requests were based on "need" or "teachers' demands." One drawback of the measure, however, is that it is sensitive only to past changes in the factors mentioned above. A subunit director will have knowledge of anticipated adjustments in prices, state regulations, enrollments, etc., which will also influence the magnitude of his request. In any event it proved impossible to obtain the needed requisition data. It was finally necessary to make use of the latest available spending data, spending in $t-1$ (CS_i). This particular measure, besides being insensitive to anticipated changes, can be affected by such extraneous factors as the cancelling of appropriations in a year for which revenues were less than anticipated. However, it is not necessarily hampered by the fact that the appropriation for $t-1$ acts as an upper limit. A subunit's consumable spending may be augmented by sacrificing some nonconsumable spending. In addition, funds can be transferred from another area of the budget if an emergency arises. Circumstances which result in transfers should be viewed by the subunit's director as forceful environmental indicators.

This reasoning suggests that when $CA_i = CY_i$, spending information can be employed in the following manner to predict requests: Suppose spending in $t-1$ is greater than or equal to appropriations in t. This will act as a signal to increase the request for $t+1$ to a point near the value of CS_i. If no spending cue is forthcoming—that is, if spending in $t-1$ is less than current appropriations—the request will be set equal to its lower limit (which is current appropriations).

Now we turn to a discussion of the second case in which $CA_i > CY_i$; the situation in which the ith subunit received surplus appropriations for t. Provided the surplus funds are considered by the staff to be nonrecurring (the typical situation), preliminary appropriations act as a base. Out of the seven requests fitting into this category none was less than CY_i, but four were less than CA_i. For the exceptional situation in which the staff desires the surplus funds to be recurring the base is set at CA_i. Neither of the two requests in this category was less than CA_i.

As might be expected, a key environmental signal when $CA_i > CY_i$ is the surplus appropriation. The subunits receiving additional nonrecurring funds will regard the event as a favorable one and therefore will consider requesting more than the base for the coming year. Whether or not there is to be an increase will also be determined by the signals from the teachers and principals who utilize a subunit's appropriations, which in turn is measured by the spending data. If CS_i is greater than or equal to CY_i, the request should equal CA_i. Otherwise, the request will be set equal to the base. When a subunit receives additional recurring funds, its request should be set equal to CA_i—which is what actually occurred in the past.

Finally, the case in which $CA_i < CY_i$ must be considered. Here, it was found that out of thirteen such requests, one was less than CA_i and three were between CA_i and CY_i. This suggests that rent final appropriations may be the more appropriate base, it is my belief that at least those subunits whose requests for were greater than or equal to CY_i adopted CY_i as the base. reason stems from the nature of the cuts made in prelimir appropriations. They were clearly due, first of all, to the neec balance the budget in a particular year rather than to the fee

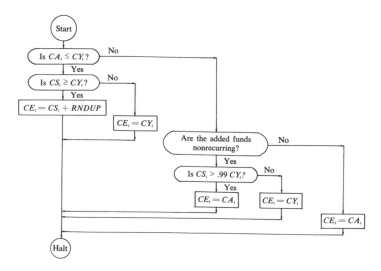

Chart 7. Requests for Consumables

that appropriations in certain areas were too high. The same percentage also tended to be removed from each subunit; not much selectivity was employed by the staff. Accordingly, there is little reason for a subunit to interpret such a cut as a permanent reduction in its base. This line of reasoning also suggests that if CS_i is greater than or equal to CY_i, its effect as an environmental signal will not be reduced. The result is that those subunits falling into the third case shall be treated as if they were affected by the same types of considerations as when $CA_i = CY_i$.

The Model for Consumable Requests

A detailed flow chart of the consumable request formulation process appears in Chart 7. First an inquiry is made to see whether $CA_i \le CY_i$. If not, those subunits which received recurring funds are separated from those that received nonrecurring funds. The requests of the former group (CE_i) are set equal to CA_i. For the latter a comparison of CS_i and CY_i is made. If $CS_i > .99\ CY_i$, then the request prediction is CA_i; otherwise it is CY_i. The parameter was estimated by running the model using a few alternatives and choosing the value which resulted in the smallest errors.

When $CA_i \leq CY_i$, spending in $t-1$ is compared to the current preliminary appropriation. If $CS_i \geq CY_i$, then the request prediction is CS_i plus an amount ($RNDUP$) that rounds CS_i up to the nearest thousand. Rounding upward in the model reflects a tendency uncovered in the interviews and borne out by an examination of the data. A parameter value of 1000 used in the rounding procedure was determined in the manner discussed above. Finally, if $CS_i < CY_i$, the request is set equal to CY_i.

In order to obtain an idea of the value of the model four alternative naive forecasts were run. These were: (1) $CE_i = CY_i$; (2) $CE_i = CA_i$; (3) $CE_i = CS$; and (4) $CE_i = CG_i$, where CG_i is the request of the ith subunit in year t's budget. Table 27 displays the previously defined yearly and overall percentage error measures for all five theories. It reveals that the model performs

Table 27—Errors of Request Predictions

Budget	CY_i	CG_i	CA_i	CS_i	Model
1961	10.8%	9.9%	13.3%	13.4%	6.1%
1962	7.9	13.8	7.9	11.7	8.1
1963	11.6	9.7	6.5	16.5	5.3
1964	11.2	10.2	17.2	17.7	9.6
1965	13.4	11.3	13.4	25.9	13.4
Overall	11.1%	11.0%	11.8%	17.4%	8.7%

slightly better on an overall basis than all the naive methods except CS_i, which it considerably outperforms. It is not the best method for 1962 and 1965, although it does not miss by much, especially in the former year.

The major discrepancies in the model's predictions can be accounted for by examining the seven errors greater than $10,000. Two are explained by the fact that vocational education responded to the environmental signals resulting from a survey of its curriculum. Two were due to the determination of a particular subunit director to request an amount he considered necessary regardless of the consequences. One resulted from the establishment of a new program. It was not possible to account for the remaining two discrepancies.

It is also useful to examine the extent to which the model is able to predict the occurrences of increases. They are hypothesized to come about when $CS_i \geq CY_i$ and $CA_i \leq CY_i$, or when $CS_i > .99CY_i$ and $CA_i > CY_i$. They may also arise in the exceptional situation in which recurring surplus funds are budgeted. Of the seventy-nine consumable requests for $t+1$ forty-eight were greater than the preliminary appropriation for t. Twenty-one of these increases (about 44 percent) can be explained by the two major hypothesized conditions. There were only six instances in which the two conditions were met and no increase was requested. On this basis the relation between CS_i and CY_i is revealed to be an important factor in determining when to enlarge a request. It was also found that among the twenty-one correctly predicted instances, twelve actual amounts were greater than the predicted amounts, five were equal, and four below. It appears that one source of error in the model may be an underestimation of the amount of increase.

Of the twenty-seven increases not explained by the relation between CS_i and CY_i only two are associated with the presence of surplus recurring funds. Hence, another source of error is a lack of knowledge of all the important environmental cues. As explained previously, this error could probably be reduced if it were possible to measure anticipations.

Requests for Nonconsumables

It was demonstrated in Table 26 that requests for nonconsumables are less dependent upon the current preliminary appropriation than requests for consumables. Further evidence of a difference in their formulation is provided by using the theory developed in the previous sections to predict nonconsumables. For the budgets from 1961 to 1965, the yearly error measure has values of 37.2, 25.5, 26.6, 18.3, and 27.5 respectively, while the overall error measure is 26.7. Hence, other considerations must be found to explain these requests.

The first step is to change the symbols being used from CA_i, CY_i, and CS_i to NA_i, NY_i, and NS_i in order to emphasize that we are dealing with the nonconsumable portion of a subunit's appropriations and spending. Also, NR_i will be defined as the actual nonconsumable request of the ith subunit for $t+1$, and it should be understood that in the following discussion the terms *request, appropriation,* and *spending* refer to the nonconsumable component.

There were twenty-six observations in the $NA_i > NY_i$ category, of which thirteen had $NR_i < NA_i$ and only two had $NR_i < NY_i$. As a result, NY_i is considered to be the base.

Of the twenty-six, there were three observations for which the surplus funds were considered by the staff to be recurring. In two of these circumstances NR_i was found to be equal to NA_i as expected. In the third, NR_i was less than NA_i, but an amount equal to the difference was used to increase the consumable request. Once a subunit received both nonrecurring and recurring funds, but since this was an extraordinary circumstance the effect on the subsequent request was not analyzed.

The remaining twenty-two observations were associated with distributions of nonrecurring surplus funds. A comparison with the same type of process for consumables reveals an important difference. The range of NA_i/NY_i was from 1.25 to 4.03, while the range of CA_i/CY_i was from 1.05 to 1.83.[4] Obviously, there is a tendency to grant larger surpluses in the former case. This is important because it is associated with a tendency for NR_i/NY_i to decrease toward a value of 1.00 as NA_i/NY_i increases. In other words, the influence of the signal represented by $NA_i > NY_i$ seems to vary inversely with the magnitude of the signal.

[4] The calculations disregard three nonconsumables for which $NY_i = 0$ and one consumable for which $CY_i = 0$.

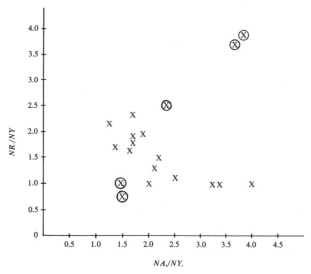

Figure 3. Saturation Effect

In order to explain this phenomenon, it was assumed that surplus funds are a favorable cue which lead subunit directors to consider an increase in their request. The extent of the increase, however, is also determined by signals from the teachers and principals who utilize the subunit's appropriations. These signals are associated with the value of NA_i/NY_i. Large values of NA_i as compared to NY_i tend to absorb immediate needs of teachers and principals, thereby causing them to apply less pressure on subunit directors for increases in requests relative to the base. This tendency has been termed a "saturation" effect.

In order to investigate the saturation effect in more detail, NR_i/NY_i versus NA_i/NY_i was plotted for the nineteen observations with $NY_i \neq 0$. (Figure 3.) With certain exceptions (the circled x points), NR_i/NY_i is at least as great as NA_i/NY_i when the latter is < 2.02; NR_i/NY_i lies between NA_i/NY_i and 1.00 when $2.02 \leq NA_i/NY_i < 3.27$; and $NR_i/NY_i = 1.00$ when $NA_i/NY_i \geq 3.27$. Some statistical justification for this tendency of NR_i/NY_i to decrease as NA_i/NY_i increases can be found by fitting a regression line to the eleven noncircled observations with abscissa values less than 3.27. The equation of the line is:

$$NR_i/NY_i = 3.13 - 0.80\, NA_i/NY_i.$$

The slope is significant at less than the .01 level using a one-tailed t test, and 51 percent of the variation in the dependent variable is explained by the independent variable.

Since the circled x points in Figure 3 do not appear to fit with the theory, let us see if it is possible to explain them. The two in the extreme upper right are associated with subunits whose preliminary appropriations for t were less than \$10,000. It may be that the directors of these small sections see their requirements as being well above their regular appropriations so that it is difficult for surpluses to induce saturation. Moving to the left, the next exception is associated with a written justification which declares that the demand cannot be filled. Therefore, it would seem to require exceptionally large surpluses here to saturate immediate needs. No information was available to explain the next exception. The final exception exists because the subunit director decided to ask for a large increase, but in consumables instead of nonconsumables.

In view of the evidence for a saturation effect when $NA_i > NY_i$, it is reasonable to investigate whether there exists a "deprivation" effect when $NA_i < NY_i$. We would expect that when NA_i is small relative to NY_i, the piling up of unfilled requirements would cause heightened signals from teachers and principals for more appropriations. These signals would then lead the subunit's director to set his next request at a high value relative to the base. Unfortunately, there were only two observations in the $NA_i < NY_i$ category. The first had $NR_i/NY_i = 1.32$ and $NA_i/NY_i = 0.91$, while the second had values of 2.50 and 0.75 respectively. These observations do not contradict the deprivation hypothesis.

It was not possible to come to any supportable conclusions for the case in which $NA_i = NY_i$, since too many observations could not be explained by the available information. Most justifications for repair and replacement requests stem from the necessity to scrap old equipment—justifications which imply that in order to understand the formulation of these requests, something should be known about the types of equipment used by each subunit and the rates at which they wear out. Many requests for capital outlay are due to the expansion of programs in particular areas. Here, it would be necessary to find out which subunits are affected by these modifications and the nature of the items required by the changes.

There is some evidence that directors set goals in terms of particular pieces of equipment per school instead of costs per pupil. For example, the head of the audio-visual section has a list of basic items, such as projectors, record players, and transparency-makers, which he believes every school should possess. The elementary education director has formed a goal of one bioscope, one portable science table, and one set of science charts per school. Similarly, secondary science has a goal of renovating the laboratories in all the schools under its jurisdiction. Since these goals are too expensive to implement all at once, directors think in terms of outfitting a few schools at a time. For example, each year secondary science requests funds to outfit the laboratories in from two to four schools.

Requests for New Personnel

Since few requests for new personnel have been made during the years for which there is data, it has not been possible to find out a great deal about their formulation. Fortunately, there is some information on the most important one—the request for teachers. Separate requests are formulated for elementary and secondary schools. Each is developed by dividing the current pupil-teacher ratio into a forecast of the enrollment increase that will occur in September of $t+1$. Obviously, the nature of the requests implies that preliminarily at least it is desired only to maintain the status quo. Attempts to reduce the pupil-teacher ratios are made when possible during the revision sessions.

Interviews indicated that requests for teachers will usually be approved if expectations for added funds are not low. This is the result of a bargain reached between the academic and business branches of the organization. Prior to the 1964 budget, the school system waited for actual enrollment increases in September of year t before budgeting more teachers for $t+1$. This meant there was no preliminary allocation for teachers. In the 1963 budget it required a downward revision in certain appropriations to transfer funds to this account. In order to avoid a repetition it was decided to forecast enrollment increases in September of $t+1$ before September of t so that a preliminary provision for added teachers would appear in the budget.

Most other new-personnel requests are usually formulated in response to the need for decreasing work loads because of past enrollment increases and program expansions. Perhaps this is done because they can be readily justified.

Summary

This analysis of budgetary requests is far from complete but should provide some useful insights. Virtually all attention was focused on materials. The current appropriation has a greater influence on consumable as opposed to nonconsumable requests because the first requires a relatively large stable replenishment component each year. Increases in consumable requests with respect to the base are due in part to environmental stimuli emanating from teachers and principals and are reflected in the amount of spending. A second source of increase is the favorable signal received from the superintendent when surplus nonrecurring funds are allocated, provided relatively high spending exists. Surplus nonrecurring funds are also an important factor in the preparation of nonconsumable requests. But the more powerful this environmental signal the less of an effect it has on the request, since there is a tendency to absorb immediate needs, thereby reducing the signals from principals and teachers.

8
Towards a Theory of
Public Budgetary
Decision-Making

This final chapter is devoted to exploring whether a unified theory which will integrate the findings of Chapters 3, 4, and 5 can be developed. First, some general assumptions and limiting conditions will be presented. Then, if possible, the main findings of the study will be derived from them in the form of propositions. Along with each proposition, supporting evidence from the study and related literature will be presented so that the obvious danger of generalizing from a single organization's experience can be properly evaluated.[1]

Basic Assumptions of the Theory

Participants

It will be assumed that the participants in the budgetary process include: (1) an administrative unit consisting of a single individual who makes allocation decisions;[2] (2) a staff function which pre-

[1] The strategy outlined here is taken from George Caspar Homan's ideas concerning the meaning of explanation in the social sciences. See *Social Behavior: Its Elementary Forms* (New York: Harcourt, Brace and World, 1961), pp. 9–10.

[2] A single individual is assumed so that there can be no interpersonal conflict within the administrative unit to influence decision-making.

pares revenue forecasts; (3) subunits, not including the two above, and occupational groups which make requests and receive appropriations; (4) a body (for example, a legislature or lay board) which must review the contents of the budget; and (5) the state government, which imposes certain legal restrictions on the organization.

The Budget

Only the operating (general fund) budget, which is required to be balanced, will be considered. It will consist of one revenue category, and, even though decisions on revenue forecasts will fall into the domain of the propositions, no distinction will be made between various sources of funds. In addition, due to the fact that the subject of the study is dependent on the state legislature for tax increases, decisions on tax rates must be regrettably disregarded.

On the expenditure side there will be three categories: salaries and benefits, materials, and debt service. Salaries and benefits are divided into four components. The first is the salaries of current employees, which will be assumed to be governed by predetermined schedules. The remaining components arise from decisions which are part of the propositions: a net change in the number of employees, salary increases over and above any built into the schedule, and new fringe benefits.[3] Since salary increases and fringe benefits are under the control of the administrator, no collective bargaining exists in this theoretical organization. The materials category, which is included in the propositions, comprises the sum of appropriations for supplies, repairs and replacements, and new equipment. Debt service involves a given component due to the principal and interest on previously committed bond issues. It also contains a component considered in the propositions, the principal and interest on bonds decided upon during budget preparation.

Discretion is therefore assumed to be exercised in six different

---

[3] No attention will be paid to increases in existing benefits.

areas: revenue forecasts, number of employees, salary increases, new fringe benefits, materials, and new debt service.

Structure of the Budgetary Process

It will be assumed that the budget for year $t+1$ is prepared in year t. The administrator will first make a preliminary set of appropriation decisions in the areas in which he exercises discretion. Any request information upon which these choices are based is treated exogenously. Then total forecasted revenues will be compared to total preliminary appropriations. On the basis of the comparison the spending and revenue decisions will be subject to revision in order to balance the budget. This interpretation of the process's structure is characteristic both of this study and that of John P. Crecine, who developed a simulation model of budgeting in three major municipalities.[4] However, in my formulation the group that must review the budget participates in the revision phase. In the processes studied by Crecine, and perhaps in a majority of cases, review takes place after the administration has prepared a balanced budget. That this extra step is not included in the propositions should not introduce a major source of error. According to evidence collected by Crecine on his city councils, by Thomas J. Anton on state legislatures, and by H. Thomas James, James A. Kelly, and Walter I. Garms on fourteen big city school boards (including the model's), the reviewing body does not seem to exercise a great deal of decision-making power.[5] The most important

[4] John P. Crecine, "A Computer Simulation Model of Municipal Budgeting," *Management Science,* 13, no. 11 (July, 1967): 802. His study will be published by Rand McNally in spring, 1969 under the title *Governmental Problem Solving: A Computer Simulation of Municipal Economy.*

[5] Crecine, "Computer Simulation Model," pp. 805–808; Thomas J. Anton, "Roles and Symbols in the Determination of State Expenditures," *Midwest Journal of Political Science,* 11, no. 1 (February, 1967): 24; and H. Thomas James, James A. Kelly, and Walter I. Garms, *Determinants of Educational Expenditures in Large Cities of the United States* (Stanford, Calif.: Stanford University, School of Education, 1966), p. 80.

exception is undoubtedly the role of Congress in federal budgeting.

Due to the structural assumptions, a maximum of twelve decisions, an initial and a final determination in each of the six areas mentioned above, may be made in preparing the budget. However, as shall be seen, not all of these possibilities are exercised in any particular year. Only a relatively large deficit (surplus), for example, will lead to reductions (increases) in materials.

Decision-Making

It is postulated that the lack of a single, operational measure upon which to base allocation decisions leads to the development of diverse subunit goals. This, in combination with mutual dependence on limited financial resources, results in a potential conflict situation over the composition of the budget.[6] Conflict may occur among the subunits and occupational groups, but that directed against the organization as personified by the administrator is of most interest here. It is augmented by the public disclosure of allocation decisions; alleged inequities are consequently easy to find.

Basic to the formulation of the propositions is the assumption that the administrator desires to reduce conflict. This behavior may be attributed to a feeling that conflict absorbs such resources as time and energy, disrupts the existing status structure,[7] produces cognitive distortions,[8] or at some point becomes pathological.[9] The method of conflict reduction employed by the administrator will

[6] See James G. March and Herbert A. Simon, *Organizations* (New York: John Wiley, 1958), pp. 121–123.

[7] *Ibid.,* p. 131.

[8] Robert R. Blake and Jane S. Mouton, "The Intergroup Dynamics of Win-Lose Conflict and Problem-Solving Collaboration in Union-Management Relations," in *Intergroup Relations and Leadership,* ed. Muzafer Sherif (New York: John Wiley, 1962), pp. 102–103.

[9] Kenneth Boulding, "A Pure Theory of Conflict Applied to Organizations," in *The Frontiers of Management Psychology,* ed. George Fisk (New York: Harper and Row, 1964), p. 47.

vary, depending upon whether the decision to be made concerns a review of previously adopted decisions or whether it involves items for which appropriations have not yet been set.

In the latter situation conflict will be *resolved* in a bargaining process. The administrator will exchange policy commitments, the financial implications of which are reflected in the budget, for the continued effective participation of the organization's subunits and occupational groups.[10] Another important bargaining resource, perhaps more appropriate for the occupational groups than the subunits, is the possibility of adding to conflict by disrupting the functioning of the organization. Others might include matching federal funds for appropriations in certain areas or the availability of a regular communication link with the administrator. In view of the many types of resources available it seems appropriate to treat the bargaining process in a flexible manner so that it embraces the use of persuasion as well as power.

In dealing with the review of previously made decisions it is clear that they must result from past bargains. Here, conflict *avoidance* will be the strategy adopted by the administrator; that is, an attempt will be made to avoid the renegotiation of these agreements in order to avoid arousing the subunits and occupational groups. An important exception dealing with extraordinary materials appropriations will be discussed below. Aaron Wildavsky has revealed another, independent motivation for avoiding the renegotiation of existing agreements. He argues that the limited information-processing capabilities of individuals lead them to review intensively only those items representing changes from the past.[11]

[10] See Richard M. Cyert and James G. March, *A Behavioral Theory of the Firm* (Englewood Cliffs, N.J.: Prentice-Hall, 1963), pp. 29–32.

[11] Aaron Wildavsky, *The Politics of the Budgetary Process* (Boston: Little, Brown and Co., 1964), pp. 8–16.

Towards a Process-Oriented Theory

Preliminary Revenue Forecasts

Proposition 1: Initially, revenue forecasts for $t+1$ will be biased downwards.

The requirement of a balanced budget insures that projected revenues must be allocated to a budgetary commitment of one form or another. As has been stated, once these commitments are made the administrator will be reluctant to revise them. If actual revenues turn out to be less than anticipated, however, he will have no choice but to make expenditure reductions. Therefore, by underestimating revenues he reduces the possibility of conflict when budgetary payments are due.

The tendency for revenue estimates developed in organizations to be biased in the direction of values that have relatively favorable consequences, in this case the reduction of conflict, has been noted in other contexts. In an experimental situation Richard M. Cyert, James G. March, and William H. Starbuck found that subjects taking the role of salesman tended to underestimate sales forecasts.[12] The experimenters attributed this behavior to the organization's preference for underestimates to overestimates when actual sales are determined.

The evidence for Proposition 1 from the foregoing study is far from conclusive but does support the hypothesized tendencies. An important source of uncertainty in the revenue forecasts is the effect of local economic conditions on certain tax bases.[13] Using regression analysis, but fitting the points by eye due to a lack of data, information on how local economic conditions (independent variable) affects the estimation of these tax bases (dependent variable) was examined. The dependent variable was measured by the change in preliminary revenue forecasts from one year to another, since there

---

[12] Cyert and March, *Behavioral Theory*, pp. 67–71.

[13] Specifically, the earned income, personal property, and mercantile tax bases.

were no adjustments in tax rates over the years studied. In order to measure the independent variable a monthly, seasonally adjusted index of general business activity for the metropolitan area was used. The numerical values were determined by calculating the trend in the index during the months prior to the determination of the preliminary forecasts. It was found that the calculated regression lines had negative intercepts, implying that the index trend must have some positive value before no downward adjustment in forecasts will be made. It appears, for example, that a positive trend of 6½ points is necessary before an increase is projected for the earned income tax. This is a fairly sizeable amount; the largest absolute value of the trend over the five years studied was 15 points. These findings also conform to the independently expressed opinions of one of the persons interviewed.

Determination of the Base

According to Wildavsky, a federal agency's budget has a "base" component representing items that the participants in the process expect to be ongoing and which is therefore not subject to critical examination.[14] As might be expected, this concept also plays an important role in the following propositions concerning materials and personnel. Before these propositions can be discussed, however, it is necessary to explain the manner in which the base has been operationalized in this study.

Previously it was noted that preliminary materials appropriations may be revised when a relatively large surplus or deficit is in the making. Since these adjustments arise out of circumstances peculiar to a particular year, they will not ordinarily be considered as arising from agreements which cannot subsequently be renegotiated. In fact, when the environment returns to normal, such revisions are expected to disappear. Accordingly, in the propositions only the preliminary component of year t's appropriations for materials is

---

[14] Wildavsky, *Politics of the Budgetary Process,* p. 17.

considered to be derived from a firm commitment; it is therefore assumed to be the base.

The situation is different when the number of personnel is considered. It should be assumed that the final decisions on employees are at least as binding as those for preliminary materials. The relative firmness in commitments arises from several factors, including its contribution to employees' morale, effective recruiting, and the mitigation of union activity. One consequence is that where the current preliminary and final numbers of employees in the budget differ, the latter as opposed to the former will be regarded as taking precedence. The only qualification on the firmness of year t's final budgeted value should occur when it differs from the actual number of employees at the start of budget preparation for $t+1$. If, for example, individuals have been recently hired to meet some emergency, the current number of employees will be larger than that finally budgeted for t; since stability in personnel decisions is necessary, this more recent figure will take precedence. Therefore, it shall be assumed that the participants in the process use the number of current employees as the base.

Others who have operationalized the concept of the base have used appropriations in t. It is well to point out that in most years preliminary materials appropriations should equal final materials appropriations and the current number of employees should equal the number finally budgeted for t. Thus, the distinction between the two definitions is not a major one. However, it should be kept in mind when later in this chapter the empirical results of this study are compared to the results of other studies.

Preliminary Decisions on Materials and Personnel

The following assertions will be found useful in setting the stage for this part of the theory:[15]

---

[15] An assertion refers to a secondary as opposed to a more significant proposition.

Assertion 1A: A materials request for $t+1$ will tend to be no less than preliminary appropriations for t.

Assertion 1B: A personnel request for $t+1$ will tend to be no less than the current number of employees.

Assertion 2A: Preliminary materials appropriations for $t+1$ will tend to be no greater than the request for $t+1$.

Assertion 2B: The preliminary number of employees budgeted for $t+1$ will tend to be no greater than the request for $t+1$.

In bargaining situations neither side will give up something for nothing. Thus, a subunit will not ask for less than has already been firmly agreed upon, while the administrator will not allocate more than is requested. It is expected that these assertions will only be violated when a suitable exchange can be arranged among the participants. For example, a subunit whose funds must temporarily be cut off from the capital budget may be pacified to some extent by a token payment from operating funds in excess of its request.

In this study twenty-three materials accounts were examined over five years for a total of 115 observations, while fifteen personnel accounts were analyzed over the same period for a total of 75. In regard to Assertions 1A and 1B, only ten materials requests for $t+1$ (9 percent) were less than year t's preliminary appropriations, while no indication could be found of a request to eliminate current employees. Supporting evidence comes from Anton, who claims that, "very few responsible [state] agency administrators will be likely to request less money than is currently available to them."[16] The reason given is that no official wants to suggest that his agency is not significant or that he is incompetent, two factors that undoubtedly could seriously affect an administrator's bargaining potential. Related evidence has also been compiled by Richard F. Fenno, Jr., provided one is willing to accept a comparison between Congress and the hypothetical administrative unit. Since both units have the primary decision-making responsibility in their respective situations, the comparison seems justified. Fenno's data

[16] Anton, "Roles and Symbols," p. 28.

refer to actions taken by the House Appropriations Committee on thirty-six domestic bureaus over the period from 1947 to 1962, a total of 576 observations in all. He determined that approximately 16 percent of all requests were less than appropriations for t.[17] This behavior conforms to the tendency expressed in Assertions 1A and 1B, but perhaps not as markedly as desired. The reason may be due to the influence of the Bureau of the Budget, which seems to act as a constraining force on federal agency requests.[18]

In regard to Assertions 2A and 2B only two of year $t+1$'s preliminary materials decisions (2 percent) were found to involve more than was requested, and no cases could be found in which employees were budgeted over the number requested. Similarly, Fenno determined that only 8 percent of the House Committee's decisions represented increases over the amounts requested.[19]

> *PROPOSITION 2A:* That portion of a materials request for $t+1$ which is equal to preliminary appropriations for t will tend to be preliminarily approved.
>
> *PROPOSITION 2B:* That portion of a personnel request for $t+1$ which is equal to the current number of employees will tend to be preliminarily approved.

These propositions are analogous to Wildavsky's findings that Congress will not intensively review an agency's budgetary base.[20] They follow directly from the assumption that any attempt by the administrator to renegotiate firmly made budgetary agreements will lead to organizational conflict. Also, since year t's preliminary materials appropriations and the current number of employees typically account for the major fraction of a subunit's request, approving this amount alleviates a large portion of the administrator's information-processing burden. In the foregoing study it was

[17] Richard F. Fenno, Jr., *The Power of the Purse: Appropriation Politics in Congress* (Boston: Little, Brown and Co., 1966), p. 357.

[18] Wildavsky, *Politics of the Budgetary Process*, p. 23.

[19] Fenno, *Power of the Purse*, p. 353.

[20] Wildavsky, *Politics of the Budgetary Process*, p. 17.

found that only sixteen materials allocations (14 percent) were less than preliminary appropriations for t, and ten of these (9 percent of the total) involved requests which were also smaller. No conflicting evidence could be found for Proposition 2B, since the salaries of all current employees are filled in automatically by the accounting department. Additional support for the propositions comes from James, Kelly, and Garms, who conclude that the policy of big city school districts is "to assume that existing programs will continue and to focus attention on proposed changes in or additions to the existing program."[21] More directly, Fenno found a relatively high 27 percent of the decisions he investigated were decreases below appropriations in t, but 59 percent of these (16 percent of the total) involved requests less than appropriations in t.[22] Incidentally, it appears from this study and Fenno's that a request for less than the amount currently budgeted (preliminarily in the former) may act in a high proportion of instances as a signal for a further cut by the reviewer. This occurred for three out of ten of this study's materials observations and fifty-four out of ninety-one of Fenno's observations.[23] On the other hand, Crecine included in his model a routine which preliminarily approves all requests less than appropriations in t.[24]

> *Corollary 1A:* A materials request for $t+1$ equal to preliminary appropriations for t will be preliminarily approved.
> *Corollary 1B:* A request for personnel equal to the current number of employees will be preliminarily approved.

In this study all twenty-six such materials requests were approved. All instances in which no new personnel were requested were automatically approved as explained before. Fenno found

---

[21] James, Kelly, and Garms. *Determinants of Educational Expenditures,* p. 91.

[22] Fenno, *Power of the Purse,* p. 357.

[23] *Ibid.*

[24] Crecine, "Computer Simulation Model," p. 798. My model displays the same decision-making behavior because it introduces negligible errors.

the same tendency although not a marked one: thirteen approvals out of twenty requests.[25] On the other hand, Crecine's mayor preliminarily handles requests equal to year t's appropriations in the same manner as requests greater than this amount.[26] The particular method will be discussed shortly.

It now remains to be discussed how that portion of a request greater than the base will be handled by the administrator. The discussion up to now has implied that the tendency will be neither to add to it at one extreme (Assertions 2A and 2B) nor to remove a larger amount at the other extreme (Propositions 2A and 2B).

> *PROPOSITION 3A:* The preliminary decision on the remaining portion of the materials request for $t+1$ will be affected by the interaction of the subunit's ability to exert influence and the magnitude of the preliminary revenue forecasts.

Assuming that the subunits can obtain information which enables them to develop expectations of the magnitude of revenues in the coming year, it may be concluded that when revenue forecasts and, correspondingly, subunit expectations are on the low side, perceived joint dependence on resources is increased.[27] As a consequence, influence attempts in the negotiation process will be intensified and will affect the administrator's judgment. In this situation the distribution of financial resources over and above year t's preliminary appropriations will reflect the relative ability of each subunit to exert influence. This ability depends upon the particular bargaining resources of each subunit, examples of which were specified earlier. When revenue forecasts are high, perceived mutual dependence is decreased. The subunits will be less motivated to exercise their influence and the administrator will be particularly attentive to each subunit's goals as reflected in its requests. In short, the magnitude of the revenue forecasts and the ability of the subunits to exert in-

---

[25] Fenno, *Power of the Purse,* p. 358.

[26] Crecine, "Computer Simulation Model," p. 798.

[27] The arguments for this proposition have their roots in March and Simon, *Organizations,* p. 126.

fluence interact, since the importance of the second variable is diminished when the first has a relatively high value. Cyert and March have discussed a similar process in which business firms distribute excess financial resources in boom periods, only to use them as the basis for cuts during downturns. They have termed such payments "organizational slack."[28]

Some support for Proposition 3A is obtained from this study. Revenue forecasts are not available when preliminary decisions are made. Therefore, it was necessary to develop an index which measures the intuitive notions of the staff as to the availability of revenues in the coming year. The index which classifies availability as being either "high" (h) or "low" (l) is based on the same information used in arriving at the intuitive notions. No attempt was made to develop a measure of the ability of the organization's subunits to influence budgetary decisions, since attempts to measure influence have not met with a great deal of success in the past.[29] Instead, with the aid of administrative personnel, twenty-three materials accounts studied individually were classified into three priority levels: L_1 (the most favored), L_2 (the next most favored), and L_3 (the least favored).

For each of these accounts all instances in the 1961 through 1965 budgets in which the request for the budget year ($t+1$) was greater than preliminary appropriations in the previous year (t) were isolated. Then the ratio of preliminary appropriations in $t+1$ to preliminary appropriations in t was calculated for each budget. This ratio measures how much a subunit obtains as compared to how much it already has. Next, the ratios were classified into the six priority-expectations cells: L_1h, L_2h, L_3h, L_1l, L_2l, and L_3l.

A statistical test for the presence of the expectations effect (not considering the priority system) was highly significant. In other words, the ratios in the three high cells were significantly larger than those in the three low cells. In examining the priority effect

[28] Cyert and March, *Behavioral Theory*, pp. 36–38.

[29] Dorwin Cartwright, "Influence, Leadership, Control," in *Handbook of Organizations*, ed. James G. March (Chicago: Rand McNally, 1965), p. 26.

independently of expectations, a statistically significant difference between the second and third levels was found, indicating that the former's ratios were larger than the latter's. There was no significant difference between the first and second levels. The results of these three tests were attributed mainly to the very low values in cell L_3l.

Differences among individual cells were examined next, revealing the following tendencies (which were not statistically significant) in the data: (1) the first priority is unaffected by expectations; (2) when expectations are low, the second priority's ratios fall relative to those of the first and the third priority's ratios fall relative to those of the second; and (3) when expectations are high, the second priority's ratios rise to the level of those of the first and the third priority's ratios almost rise to that level. In short, there is a tendency for the priority effect to be blurred when expectations are high and to be pronounced when they are low.

It was also possible to study the priority and expectations effects on the number of requests which have been approved and the number of requests which have been cut. It was statistically verified that the chances of approving a request in high years was significantly greater than the chances of approving a request in low years, and that the chances of approving a request increase as the priority level of a subunit is raised. The first finding provides evidence for an observation of James G. March and Herbert A. Simon which was used in the argument for Proposition 3A. They claim that when a resource is relatively unlimited, organizations tend not to challenge subgroup claims on it.[30]

> *PROPOSITION 3B:* When revenue expectations are low, cautiousness will lead the administrator to preliminarily approve few, if any, requests for added personnel; the ability to influence will have little effect. When revenue expectations are high, the relative ability of subunits to influence the

---

[30] March and Simon, *Organizations,* p. 126.

administrator will be effective, since cautiousness will not be as important a factor.

The discussion of preliminary decisions on requests for additional employees assumes as before that two crucial variables will be revenue anticipations and a particular subunit's ability to exert influence. It is also expected that the administrator will display a relatively cautious attitude towards increasing employees, since he is aware that approvals must be considered as long-term commitments on his part. This will be reflected in a more stringent policy towards the approval of new personnel as opposed to materials increases.

In order to analyze the effects of these factors, an assignment of new-personnel accounts to priorities was made on the same basis as for materials. Then the proportion of requests preliminarily allocated to each priority in both high and low-expectations years was calculated. Expectations appeared to be a factor, since each of the top two priorities received a larger proportion of their requests for high as opposed to low years. This could not be determined for the third priority because it made no requests in low years. The priority effect seemed to exist, since when expectations were high, the first group did better than the second, which in turn did better than the third—assuming the elimination from the second group of one subunit which consistently asked for very large amounts, little of which were ever preliminarily approved. Also, when expectations were low, the first priority was not treated worse than the second. Whether the second did at least as well as the third could not be determined because of the indeterminacy problem. The relative caution in dealing with new-personnel requests as compared to materials was highlighted by the fact that when expectations were low, none were approved; when expectations were high, only the first priority tended to get all of its requests approved.

The evidence from other sources is not necessarily consistent with Propositions 3A and 3B. In Crecine's model the mayor's preliminary decision on a request greater than or equal to appropriations in t is based on a linear function of the subunit's request, budgetary, and spending data.[31] It appears that a completely different mechanism is at work here, since neither priorities, expectations, nor cautiousness in personnel decisions are explicitly considered. However, it is possible that at least the first two factors could be revealed in an analysis of the parameters of the decision functions. Fenno has presented evidence of priority systems in the decisions of the House Appropriations Committee. He developed two different rankings based on appropriations as a percentage of requests and on an average yearly growth rate in appropriations. The latter ranking, more related to this study since it is based on appropriation increases, ran almost continuously from 23 percent for the Office of Education to -0.5 percent for the Bureau of Public Debt.[32] However, there is no consideration of revenue expectations and caution in approving new employees in Fenno's discussion. Finally, Otto A. Davis, M.A.H. Dempster, and Aaron Wildavsky have found that Congress's decisions on many domestic agencies' budgets can be represented by linear, stochastic decision rules. In particular, a fixed percentage of the request plus a random error of not unreasonable magnitude suffices for fifty-three out of sixty-six agencies investigated. However, there does not appear to be any evidence that Congress actually acts in this manner; only that it acts as if the rules were true.[33] The distinction is crucial, since the propositions discussed here are intended to explain actual decision-making.

Salary Increases

Fundamental to the propositions that will be developed concerning salary increases is the assumption that employees make salary

---

[31] Crecine, "Computer Simulation Model," pp. 801–802.

[32] Fenno, *Power of the Purse,* pp. 366–410.

[33] Otto A. Davis, M. A. H. Dempster, and Aaron Wildavsky, "A Theory of the Budgetary Process," *American Political Science Review,* 60, no. 3 (September, 1966): 531.

comparisons. This is an accepted fact in public administration as well as other areas.[34] Therefore, it was not surprising to find that teachers' groups in the model's school system collect comparison information. The implication for administrators is that a potential exists for an adverse effect on morale. Employees will react unfavorably toward comparisons which show that individuals with similar characteristics are receiving higher pay. This follows from one of the basic laws of "social justice" and has been empirically verified in the case of blue-collar workers by Martin Patchen.[35] Since budgetary information in the public sector is so readily available, it would be expected that these tendencies would be even more pronounced there. As a result, it may be concluded that public employees, when bargaining for salary increases, have an important resource—their discontent—to which the administrator in his capacity as conflict-reducer will be especially sensitive.

One consequence of this sensitivity is the widespread use of classification plans (salary schedules) in order to insure the same pay for similar work. For this reason it was assumed that each occupation in the hypothetical organization has its own schedule in which are determined not only minimums and maximums but also the levels between these limits. A salary increase is considered to be the result of raising the amounts in all the cells of a particular schedule. In addition, it seems safe to conclude that the equal pay for equal work norm will result in all employees under the same schedule receiving increases at the same time. Consequently, a "group consciousness" is fostered among the individuals in particular occupations. This feeling of togetherness is strengthened by

[34] For example, see Herbert A. Simon, Donald W. Smithburg, and Victor A. Thompson, *Public Administration* (New York: Alfred A. Knopf, 1950), p. 360; William G. Bowen, *The Wage-Price Issue: A Theoretical Analysis* (Princeton, N.J.: Princeton University Press, 1960), pp. 139–141; and Paul Pigors and Charles A. Myers, *Personnel Administration*, 4th ed. (New York: McGraw-Hill, 1961), p. 366.

[35] See Homans, *Social Behavior*, pp. 72–78; and Martin Patchen, *The Choice of Wage Comparisons* (Englewood Cliffs, N.J.: Prentice-Hall, 1961), Chap. 5.

the existence of employee associations, also differentiated by occupation, one of whose functions may be to present salary increase requests at budget preparation time.

Thus, while dissatisfaction within groups is not an important consideration for the administrator, competition between groups for the organization's limited financial resources *is* an important factor. It is expected that this competition will be fostered by intergroup salary comparisons. Yet, because of occupational differences, it does not seem appropriate that they will be based on salary levels; instead comparisons are expected to be based on salary increases. In particular, any given group will be especially sensitive to situations in which some other group receives raises and it does not. Therefore, the administrator in his capacity as a conflict-reducer will act according to the following rule:

> *PROPOSITION 4A:* Salary increases will tend to be granted to all employee groups at the same time.

Data from the school study seem to bear out the proposition, although gaps exist in some nonteaching occupations' salary-increase history. From the 1954 to the 1965 budget four increases initiated by the school district were granted to all employees insofar as can be told. In addition, two increases for teachers initiated by the state legislature induced the district to provide for all or at least most other personnel. On a few occasions, however, groups with industrial counterparts received raises to keep pace with wages in the local labor market. Particular groups, excluding those with industrial counterparts, received raises twice, but these resulted from schedule structure modifications.

Unfortunately, the administrator is usually unable to thwart the pervasiveness of the comparison phenomenon so easily. It is still possible for employee groups to make interorganizational comparisons with similar occupations in other public institutions and to become discontented as a consequence. The administrator faces a more difficult task here, since only the salaries of his own organization are under control. In order to solve this problem he will become especially sensitive to the dissatisfaction of that group which has the greatest potential for disrupting the organization. This "controlling" occupation (in the sense that it can regulate conflict) will be teachers in local school districts and perhaps public safety employees in municipalities. For the purpose of measuring their dissatisfaction, the administrator also will resort to interorganizational comparisons.

> *PROPOSITION 4B:* A salary increase will be granted when interorganizational comparisons reveal that the salary structure of the controlling occupation has approached some critical level.

Since in this study the controlling occupation is teachers, a list of seventeen comparable districts was determined with the aid of the school district's personnel department. Three criteria were used for selection: enrollment of at least 50,000 pupils, a city as opposed to a county district, and location in the same quadrant of the country as the model's system. A particular salary, the starting salary for teachers with a bachelor's degree, was chosen to represent the entire teachers' schedule. Then this salary was compiled for all the selected districts for the school years 1953/54 to 1964/65. A review of the data revealed that all entries were made just before the model's district made its decision. It was found that a salary increase was granted when and only when no other district had a starting salary below the model's (four occasions).

While this evidence indicates that decisions are made using comparisons, it does not show that the motivation stems from an attempt to mitigate employee dissatisfaction. Subsequent research may substantiate this claim, but it appears that other factors, such as recruitment pressures, may play at least as important a role. Charles S. Benson, for example, has attributed salary raises in school districts to a comparison process, but on the grounds that they attempt in this manner to attract high-quality teachers.[36]

---

[36] Charles S. Benson, *The Economics of Public Education* (Boston: Houghton Mifflin, 1961), pp. 415–423.

James, Kelly, and Garms see competition in the local labor market and in other large cities in the nation as one important consideration influencing salary increases for teachers in big city districts.[37]

New Debt Service

It is expected that the administrator will be reluctant to issue new bonds, thereby increasing the level of debt service in the operating budget. For one reason this action would put a further restriction on the allocations to subunits and occupational groups, thus increasing the possibility of conflict. Instead, he will first attempt to meet payments on capital projects from other sources which have little or no effect on the operating budget, such as temporarily idle cash balances or short-term bank loans. When it appears, however, that the value of contracts outstanding is high and alternate methods of financing must be repaid, there is no recourse but to plan to issue new bonds. The administrator can measure the demands of these financial obligations from information contained in the balance sheet of the bond fund.

> *PROPOSITION 5:* New debt service will be budgeted when the pressure of the bond fund's financial obligations reaches some critical level.

In this study a measure of financial pressure was developed which closely resembled the working capital of the bond fund after the start of operating budget preparation. The measure was able to distinguish between no new debt service and some new debt service in the ten budgets from 1956 to 1965. The measure's values for the three budgets in which new debt service appeared were considerably lower than its values for the budgets with no such provisions. The measure had some difficulty, however, in predicting whether bonds should be issued at the beginning of $t+1$ (some financial pressure) or the end of t (severe financial pressure).

[37] James, Kelly, and Garms, *Determinants of Educational Expenditures,* pp. 63–64.

Balancing the Budget: Deficits

Once the decisions discussed above have been made the administrator will compare the value of the initial revenue forecasts with total appropriations up to this point in the process. Let us suppose that on this basis a deficit is projected for $t+1$. According to the foregoing postulates he will balance the budget with a set of actions that in his judgment will produce the least turmoil in the organization. In order to accomplish his objective he must first locate a suitable area in the budget, then determine the extent to which the area can be affected, and finally, if necessary, move on to the next most suitable area. This type of process is also used by Crecine.[38]

> *PROPOSITION 6A:* If a deficit exists, an attempt will first be made to balance the budget without immediately affecting existing agreements (including those made in the preliminary phase).

The hypothetical administrator is interested in solving pressing problems and does not attach a great deal of significance to the implications of his solutions for the uncertain future.[39] Consequently, he will seek out areas in the budget which, if used for balancing purposes, will not produce conflict immediately, though they may at some future time. Consider, for example, the reinvestigation of the initial revenue forecasts to see if they may be raised to more optimistic levels. This policy will not lead to any immediate dissatisfaction on the part of the subunits and employee groups, but does involve the risk of having to forfeit obligations if actual revenues turn out to be less than anticipated.

It must be pointed out that the forecasts will not be pushed upwards without justification simply for expediency's sake. It is expected that a reexamination of the information used in making projections and a search for additional data to see if the projections may be raised to values with a lower but reasonable subjective

---

[38] Crecine, "Computer Simulation Model," pp. 803–804.
[39] See Cyert and March, *Behavioral Theory,* pp. 118–120.

probability of occurring will be made. This interpretation seems especially appropriate in view of the earlier claim that revenue forecasts will initially be biased downwards.

Another crucial factor determining the limits to which forecasts will be raised are expectations about the magnitude of revenues for the years immediately following the coming one. If these expectations are encouraging there will be more of a tendency to raise forecasts than if they are disappointing. The reason is that, if cuts must be made when actual revenues are determined, the administrator can expect at that time to have arguments which will convince the subunits that restorations will be made soon.

Another strategy compatible with Proposition 6A involves the use of appropriations for capital projects.[40] Preliminarily, especially when revenue expectations for the coming year are high, some portion, however small, of these appropriations would be expected to be included in the operating budget in order to save interest costs. Yet when a deficit is in the making, it is possible to transfer them back to the capital budget. As a consequence, operating obligations are still met, except from a different source, and the possibility of conflict at some future time over the content of the capital budget is increased (although the amount of transferred funds may be a small fraction of the total available for capital projects). In short, capital appropriations may be considered a form of organizational slack, since increases in abundant years serve as the basis for cuts in lean years.

It seems safe to conclude that, if necessary, all appropriations for capital projects in the operating budget will be transferred unless there exists some lesser amount above which conflict over the capital budget will occur.

PROPOSITION 6B: If a deficit remains at this point, the appropriations of subunits with the least ability to influence

---

[40] These appropriations may be considered to be requested by one of the organization's subunits and treated in the preliminary budgeting phase in the same manner as materials.

the administrator will be cut. He will continue to cut appropriations from more and more influential subunits until the
budget is balanced.

At this point there is no alternative but to make cuts in the appropriations of those subunits which can cause the least turmoil in the
organization. As indicated previously, ability to influence cannot
be easily measured; therefore, it is no easy task to specify which
units will be most susceptible to budgetary trimming. This study
suggests that those activities whose objectives are only indirectly
linked to the main purposes of the organization will tend to be
chosen. More specifically, there are some activities whose purposes
may be viewed as a means to the organization's major goals rather
than as directly contributing to them. For example, in the school
district studied health services were heavily affected by deficit-
removal procedures, since their objective of physical fitness was a
means to educational attainment rather than a direct contribution.

There are also activities which make direct contributions but
whose participants represent a special, small segment of the population. For instance, such educational activities outside the regular
day school program as evening school were heavily affected when
the need arose to cut deficits. Burton R. Clark's study of adult
education programs in California school systems corroborates this
point. He found that adult education was considered a marginal
program by the state legislature because it was not related to train-
ing children. It was the first and the most severely cut when financial
resources ran low.[41]

It is difficult to predict the extent to which each relatively un-
influential subunit will be affected, but it is doubtful that any subunit will be completely eliminated in the short run—especially
where the state requires them. According to the reasoning developed previously, it would be expected that materials appropriations

[41] Burton R. Clark, "Organizational Adaptation and Precarious Values,"
in *Complex Organizations: A Sociological Reader,* ed. Amitai Etzioni (New
York: Holt, Rinehart and Winston, 1961), pp. 163–164.

above the base and personnel added in the preliminary phase would be most affected, since they are derived from relatively tenuous agreements. For the same reason, base materials will be examined before existing personnel.

These ideas concerning impending deficits may be compared to the work of James D. Barber.[42] He was able to persuade the members of thirteen of Connecticut's local boards of finance to make hypothetical budgetary cuts in a laboratory setting. Although he did not study the decision process in great detail, various criteria used in making choices were isolated. The most frequent reason for not cutting a particular area was that it was "uncontrollable"; in other words, required by state law or the result of a previously made long-run commitment. Certain "essential" services were also considered to be in the uncontrollable category and by common agreement were not touched. This finding suggests a distinction between fringe and essential activities which is reflected in Proposition 6B. Another criterion was to concentrate on "visible" accounts representing large items or recent increases. The first type of visibility is a factor in the school district's transfer of building alteration funds, although this is not considered in Proposition 6A. A third criterion which involved reviewing those past decisions originally made with some doubt is not considered at all in the propositions.

The findings of Crecine are also relevant to this discussion.[43] His municipal budgeting model has a deficit-elimination process which consists of a priority system based on account classifications. First, maintenance, equipment, general expense, and salary accounts, in that order, are checked to remove appropriations above the mayor's prescribed limits. If the deficit is not eliminated, the nonsalary accounts are reexamined in the same order to remove all increases over the current year's appropriations. Finally, if necessary, there is a uniform reduction in all nonsalary accounts. Crecine's results correspond to Barber's in the use of a review of recent increases

---

[42] James D. Barber, *Power in Committees: An Experiment in the Governmental Process* (Chicago: Rand McNally, 1966), Chap. 2.

[43] Crecine, "Computer Simulation Model," pp. 803–804.

and to mine in the consideration of salary accounts as more or less essential appropriations. There remains sufficient discrepancy between the three sets of findings, however, to point out that further research is in order.

Balancing the Budget: Surpluses

Finally, the processes used to balance the budget when a surplus is projected for $t+1$ must be considered. This portion of the theory is not well developed, partly because public institutions seem to have little opportunity to follow this path in their decision-making. Surpluses are, however, important bargaining resources which can be exchanged by the administrator for (implied) promises of tranquility on the part of those subunits and groups which rank high on a specialized asset: the power to make a significant contribution to organizational conflict. It therefore appears that one area to which surplus appropriations are likely to flow will be the controlling occupation's compensation.

In the years between salary increases the dissatisfaction of the controlling occupation with its compensation will be building up in intensity. Since these are years in which this group's salary schedule has not yet fallen to its critical level, there are likely to be other aspects of the wage bundle about which there is more concern. As a result, it is expected that discontent will focus primarily on fringe benefits. Moreover, there will be more pressure for new benefits than for increases in existing ones, since the first represent an added responsibility upon the administrator which in time can also be increased.[44] Accordingly, it is predicted that a portion of the surplus will be used for this purpose, and, following from Proposition 4A, will be applied to all other employees as well. Before assuming this recurring obligation, however, the administrator will

[44] Arthur M. Ross, "The External Wage Structure," in *New Concepts in Wage Determination,* ed. George W. Taylor and Frank C. Pierson (New York: McGraw-Hill, 1957), p. 183.

want to check to see whether his surplus funds will be available on a recurring basis; that is, for at least one year beyond $t+1$.

> *PROPOSITION 7:* Provided a recurring surplus is forecasted for $t+1$ and the discontent of the controlling occupation is building up, new fringe benefits will be granted.

In order to measure the dissatisfaction of teachers, the number of comparable districts with lower B.A. starting salaries was used, as was done when discussing salary increases. It was assumed that dissatisfaction would be building up when this index had a value from 1 to D, where D is much smaller than 17, which is the maximum. It was found that new fringe benefits have been granted when and only when recurring surplus funds were available and the index's value was between one and four (three occasions). In addition, all employees seem to have shared in receiving them. There were occasions when existing benefits were increased, but it was not possible to discover the reasons.

Once significant problem areas are handled, the administrator will be affected by those conventional influence attempts which do not involve major threats to organizational tranquility. A technique that should prove particularly useful in securing additional appropriations is calling attention to previously made cuts in personnel and preliminary materials. Here, as with preliminary decisions, the distribution will tend to be widely shared, but will also reflect each subunit's ability to influence.

Crecine's model also incorporates a surplus-distribution process. Its content, however, is based on a priority system of account categories; the order is the reverse of that for his deficit-elimination routine. Interestingly enough, compensation increases make up the first category, provided a minimum amount can be offered, but they involve salaries, not fringe benefits.[45]

---

[45] Crecine, "Computer Simulation Model," pp. 802–803.

Summary

The propositions which have evolved from my study of budgetary decision-making can be summarized as follows:

1. Initially, revenue forecasts will be underestimated to help insure that budgetary payments can be made when actual revenues are determined.

2. New appropriations for personnel and materials will be affected by the interaction of revenue expectations and the ability of a subunit to exert influence. One added consideration for the first type of appropriation will be a relative cautiousness in making approvals owing to the firm nature of these commitments.

3. Salary increases will tend to be made for all employees at the same time and will arise out of efforts to mitigate the discontent of that occupation considered most critical for the functioning of the organization.

4. There will be a tendency to avoid as long as possible the introduction of new debt service into the operating budget, partly because it will facilitate allocations to the subunits and occupational groups, thus decreasing the chances of tension.

5. When a deficit is projected the administrator will attempt to avoid the renegotiation of existing agreements by reexamining revenue forecasts and treating capital-outlay appropriations as slack. If a deficit remains, then subunits whose functions are only indirectly linked to basic organizational purposes or which serve small segments of the population will be most affected.

6. When a surplus is projected the administrator will attempt to exchange budgetary commitments, particularly new fringe benefits, for (implied) promises of conflict reduction on the part of those groups which have the greatest potential for· controlling tension.

7. The state government will have both obvious and subtle effects on the budgetary process, depending upon the types of restrictions

it imposes. The requirement of a balanced budget will lead to search behavior on the part of the organization in order to eliminate a deficit or distribute a surplus. Where the state controls increases in the organization's revenues it will influence materials and new-personnel increases through Propositions 3A and 3B. State regulations can determine those accounts which cannot be reduced when a deficit exists. Where the state requires floors on the controlling occupation's salary schedule, any increase affecting the organization will lead to commensurate raises for all other employees.

By concentrating on the decision process, the manner in which a public administrator allocates financial resources has been analyzed. Starting from the assumption that he desires to reduce the level of conflict over the composition of the budget, certain propositions have been derived which imply that existing appropriations will not be easily reduced, while new appropriations will be determined through a bargaining process in which a crucial asset of the subunits will be their ability to add to tension. This does not mean that the possibility that other objectives also influence appropriation decisions has been rejected. It *does* imply that adherence to this particular goal explains many of this study's findings and is a suitable starting point from which a more comprehensive theory may in time evolve.

Appendices

Bibliography

Index

Appendix I
Sources of Data

Interviews conducted with the staff were an important source of information for the development of the model. It was possible to meet repeatedly with all personnel who had a hand in budget preparation except the school board members. These sessions were mainly question and answer periods, but also were used for discussing hypothetical examples and for reviewing actual decisions. It was soon apparent that information obtained in this manner could not provide a complete picture of the budgetary process because of the selective perception of the participants and their difficulty in remembering past details. Furthermore, there had been a large staff turnover in recent years.

The other important source of information consisted of various written documents including: (1) department requests; (2) letters of department heads justifying requests; (3) preliminary budgets; (4) the revisions in the preliminary budgets made during the school board review; (5) final budgets; (6) miscellaneous documents, such as letters, charts, and financial statements; and (7) newspaper articles concerning the school budget.[1] Most of this material (with the exception of numbers 3, 4, and 5) was unavailable prior to 1960 and the rest was difficult to compile.

Department requests, preliminary appropriations, and final appropriations were hard to obtain for a variety of reasons. Materials requests for a number of the business functions were not always available. Materials appropriations were hard to find because the budget, except for

---

[1] Obtained from the Pennsylvania Room of the Carnegie Library, Pittsburgh, Pa.

153

1965, does not list together all of the accounts associated with a subunit. All maintenance and capital-outlay allocations, for example, appear in special sections. New-personnel requests were hard to locate because they only appeared in letters of justification. It is impossible to know if the records examined contained all such letters or if some requests were made without providing letters. In addition, it was necessary to price all new-personnel requests that were not approved by using the salaries of similar positions in the same year as a guide. New-personnel appropriations were also hard to find. In some budgets the number of new personnel in a certain account was not given. Consequently, it was impossible to distinguish the portion of an appropriation increase due to automatic salary increases from the portion due to new personnel. Fortunately, this problem did not arise for the largest accounts. Other difficulties that arose in the collection of data were due to changes in methods of reporting information and changes in the composition of accounts.

Because of these problems, requests and appropriations could only be tabulated from the 1960 to 1965 budgets. The 1960 budget was the only budget for which the superintendent officially told department heads to hold the line on requests. Rather than build a special branch of the model to handle this single case, it was dropped from consideration. As a result, the model as a whole was tested against the data from 1961 to 1965. Information on certain important decisions, such as general salary increases, new debt service, and budget-balancing processes, was collected back to 1954 and is utilized in the chapters that discuss these decisions.

Appendix II
Calculation of the General Impressions Measure for 1961 through 1965

In order to test the theories concerning the effects of expectations on preliminary materials decisions, the 1961–1965 budget years must be classified as either "high" or "low." Some of the information required for this purpose is not available, however, since no written records of the staff's meetings to review requests were found. In particular, it is not known at what time during the summer the meetings were held or if the estimates of the magnitudes of changes that were found were the same ones used during the meetings.

Table 28—The General Impressions Measure

Budget	State legislature	Economic conditions	Carry-over	Salary increases	Total	G.I.M.
1965	$ 0	$ 200,000	$1,000,000	$ −500,000	$ 700,000	High
1964	1,000,000	˙400,000	0	−500,000	900,000	High
1963	1,000,000	−700,000	0	−500,000	−200,000	Low
1962	2,500,000	100,000	0	−2,200,000	400,000	High
1961	0	−500,000	0	−500,000	−1,000,000	Low

Table 28 provides a summary of the components of the G.I.M. for 1961 to 1965. The change made by the 1961 state legislature was the substitution of the earned income tax for the per capita tax. The house passed this bill on July 25. Department requests were due to be returned to the superintendent July 14. Since the preliminary review could not have started before this date, it seems safe to assume that the staff expected the revenue change when they held the meetings. The amount of change was estimated to be $2,500,000 for 1962. Adoption of the earned income tax also had implications for the 1963 budget, since the tax is based on the first three quarters of a year and the last quarter of the previous year. This means that the first full year's collections were not made until 1963. The added funds due to the extra quarter were estimated at $1,000,000. There is no question that this change was known to the staff when it prepared the budget.

The change made by the 1963 legislature involved adding one mill to the real estate tax rate. The house passed the bill on July 26 and department requests were due by June 30. This difference seems small enough to allow the assumption that the staff expected the change during its meetings. An amount of $1,000,000 was consequently added to the revenue estimates for 1964. The 1963 legislature also increased the parameters of the state-subsidy formula in order to compensate for mandated increases in teacher salaries. Since these added revenues and expenditures tend to cancel out, the change need not be considered.

The other components of Table 28 arise in the following manner: The effects of economic conditions were estimated by substituting the appropriate index trend value into the regression equations. During the preparation of the 1965 budget it was known that there would be a carry-over from 1963 of approximately $1,000,000. A general salary increase was considered necessary only for 1962 and was estimated to be almost $1,700,000. Finally, I deducted $500,000 in each year for automatic raises.

Appendix III
Supplementary Tables

Table 29—Characteristics of Preliminary Appropriations Ratios

Cell	Median[a]	Range	Sample size
11	1.11	1.03 – 2.32	11
12	1.20	1.03 – 4.13[b]	10
21	1.22	0.78 – 4.55[c]	19
22	1.08	0.36 – 3.50[d]	16
31	1.12	1.00 – 1.59	10
32	1.00	0.53 – 1.07[e]	9

[a]The statistical tests that investigate the location of cell distributions are nonparametric and therefore do not examine the values of any specific locational parameter. The medians are presented here in order to provide the reader with some feeling for the locations of each distribution.

[b]The second highest value was 2.21.

[c]The second highest value was 3.54, third highest was 2.50, and second lowest was 1.04.

[d]The next most extreme values were 1.72 and 0.99.

[e]The second lowest value was 0.97.

Table 30—B.A. Minimum Salaries[a]

City	Oct. 1964	Nov. 1963	Oct. 1962	Nov. 1961	Oct. 1960
Pittsburgh[b]	*$5000*	*$5000*	*$5000*	*$4300*	*$4300*
Akron	5200	5100	4800	4600	4400
Baltimore	5000	4800	4500	4500	4500
Boston	4980	4980	4740	4740	4020
Buffalo	5100	4700	4700	4500	4500
Chicago	5350	5350	5350	5100	5000
Cincinnati	4900	4800	4800	4600	4350
Cleveland	5000	5000	5000	5000	4500
Columbus	4700	4700	4700	4400	4250
Dayton	5000	4830	4700	4557	4424
Detroit	5300	5100	5100	5000	4800
Indianapolis	5000	4900	4700	4600	4460
Milwaukee	5275	5025	4900	4650	4550
Newark	5600	5300	4900	4900	4600
New York	5300	5300	5300	4800	4800
Philadelphia	5300	5300	4700	4300	4200
Toledo	4800	4600	4600	4600	4160
Washington, D. C.	5350	5000	4800	4800	4800

[a]See Chap. 4, fn. 10, for the sources of these data.

[b]The 1955 state legislature stayed in session until 1956, when it decided to grant a $400 increase in salaries in the following manner: $200 starting September 1956, $100 starting September 1957, and $100 starting September 1958. All other increases were the result of the district's initiative.

Table 31—Working Capital of the Bond Fund

Date: August 31	1964	1963	1962	1961
Current Assets:				
Cash	$ 121,443	$ 202,232	$ 912,106	$ 151,487
Receivables	0	20,000	0	0
Total (T_1)	$ 121,443	$ 222,232	$ 912,106	$ 151,487
Current Liabilities:				
Encumbrances	$ 104,479	$ 62,983	$ 134,047	$ 25,020
Contracts	834,740	2,108,314	1,454,087	1,717,399
Due other funds	129,100	1,985,005	0	1,817,000
Total (T_2)	$ 1,068,319	$ 4,156,302	$ 1,588,134	$ 3,559,419
Working Capital ($T_1 - T_2$)	$ −946,876	$ −3,934,070	$ −676,028	$ −3,407,932

Nov. 1959	Oct. 1958	Nov. 1957	Oct. 1956	Sept. 1955	Sept. 1954	Nov. 1953
$4000	*$4000*	*$3900*	*$3800*	*$3200*	*$3200*	*$3000*
4200	4000	3800	3700	3400	3400	3300
4000	4000	3600	3600	3200	3200	3000
4020	4020	3768	3504	3504	3492	3312
4000	4000	3600	3600	3600	3000	3000
5000	4350	4000	4000	3750	3400	3000
4200	4050	3900	4000	3500	3200	3200
4500	4250	4000	4000	3800	3500	3500
4150	3850	3700	3500	3350	3200	3075
4268	4050	4000	3550	3550	3400	3200
4700	4500	4500	4250	3914	3862	3706
4400	4200	4050	3800	3650	3500	3350
4200	4200	4000	3600	3527	3527	3527
4300	4000	4000	4000	3700	3700	—c
4500	4000	4000	4000	3900	3450	3000
4000	4000	3600	3600	3200	3000	3000
4160	4000	3400	3400	3400	3400	3200
4500	4500	3900	3900	3900	3440	3440

cData not available.

1960	1959	1958	1957	1956	1955
$ 1,140,950	$ 304,049	$ 3,085,027	$ 337,154	$ 2,295,860	$ 4,295,307
0	0	0	0	50,000	0
$ 1,140,950	$ 304,049	$ 3,085,027	$ 337,154	$ 2,345,860	$ 4,295,307
$ 878,060	$ 221,419	$ 92,498	$ 10,883	$ 121,257	$ 120,689
2,154,384	2,525,873	2,406,618	1,848,256	1,994,116	2,310,090
0	926,493	0	0	50,000	995
$ 3,032,444	$ 3,673,785	$ 2,499,116	$ 1,859,139	$ 2,165,373	$ 2,431,774
$ −1,891,494	$ −3,369,736	$ +585,911	$ −1,521,985	$ +180,487	$ +1,863,533

Bibliography

Anshen, Melvin. "The Federal Budget as an Instrument for Management and Analysis." In *Program Budgeting: Program Analysis and the Federal Budget,* edited by David Novick. Cambridge, Mass.: Harvard University Press, 1965, pp. 3–23.

Anton, Thomas J. "Roles and Symbols in the Determination of State Expenditures." *Midwest Journal of Political Science* 11 (1967): 27–43.

Banfield, Edward C. *Political Influence.* New York: The Free Press of Glencoe, 1961.

Barber, James D. *Power in Committees: An Experiment in the Governmental Process.* Chicago: Rand McNally & Co., 1966.

Benson, Charles S. *The Economics of Public Education.* Boston: Houghton Mifflin Co., 1961.

Blake, Robert R., and Mouton, Jane S. "The Intergroup Dynamics of Win-Lose Conflict and Problem-Solving Collaboration in Union-Management Relations." In *Intergroup Relations and Leadership,* edited by Muzafer Sherif. New York: John Wiley & Sons, Inc., 1962, pp. 94–139.

Bonini, Charles P. *Simulation of Information and Decision Systems in the Firm.* Englewood Cliffs, N.J.: Prentice-Hall, Inc., 1963.

Boulding, Kenneth. "A Pure Theory of Conflict Applied to Organizations." In *The Frontiers of Management Psychology,* edited by George Fisk. New York: Harper and Row Pubs., 1964, pp. 41–67.

Bowen, William G. *The Wage-Price Issue: A Theoretical Analysis.* Princeton, N.J.: Princeton University Press, 1960.

Braybrooke, David, and Lindblom, Charles E. *A Strategy of Decision: Policy Evaluation as a Social Process.* New York: The Free Press of Glencoe, 1963.

Buchanan, James M., and Tullock, Gordon. *The Calculus of Consent: Logical Foundations of Constitutional Democracy.* Ann Arbor, Mich.: The University of Michigan Press, 1962.

Cartter, Allan M., and Marshall, F. Ray. *Labor Economics: Wages, Employment, and Trade Unionism.* Homewood, Ill.: Richard D. Irwin, Inc., 1967.

Cartwright, Dorwin. "Influence, Leadership, Control." In *Handbook of Organizations,* edited by James G. March. Chicago: Rand McNally & Co., 1965, pp. 1–41.

Cincinnati Public Schools, Research Department. "Reports on Salary Structure of Cities over 200,000 in Population," 1953/54, 1955/56, 1956/57. Mimeographed. Cincinnati, Ohio: The Department, 1953, 1955, 1956.

Clark, Burton R. "Organizational Adaptation and Precarious Values." In *Complex Organizations: A Sociological Reader,* edited by Amitai Etzioni. New York: Holt, Rinehart and Winston, Inc., 1961, pp. 159–167.

Clarkson, Geoffrey P. E. *Portfolio Selection: A Simulation of Trust Investment.* Englewood Cliffs, N.J.: Prentice-Hall, Inc., 1962.

Cohen, Kalman J., and Cyert, Richard M. "Simulation of Organizational Behavior." In *Handbook of Organizations,* edited by James G. March. Chicago: Rand McNally & Co., 1965, pp. 305–333.

Council of State Governments. *The Book of the States, 1966–67.* Vol. 16. Chicago: The Council, 1966.

Crecine, John P. "A Computer Simulation Model of Municipal Budgeting." *Management Science* 13 (1967): 786–815.

Cyert, Richard M., and March, James G. *A Behavioral Theory of the Firm.* Englewood Cliffs, N.J.: Prentice-Hall, Inc., 1963.

Dahl, Robert A. *Who Governs? Democracy and Power in an American City.* New Haven, Conn.: Yale University Press, 1961.

Dauwalder, Donald D. *Vocational Education in the Pittsburgh Public Schools.* Pittsburgh, Pa.: The Pittsburgh Board of Public Education, 1963.

Davis, Otto A. "Empirical Evidence of 'Political' Influences Upon the Expenditure and Taxation Policies of Public Schools." In *The Public Economy of Urban Communities,* edited by Julius Margolis. Baltimore, Md.: The Johns Hopkins Press, 1965, pp. 92–111.

———; Dempster, M. A. H.; and Wildavsky, Aaron. "A Theory of the Budgetary Process." *American Political Science Review* 60 (1966): 529–547.

Dixon, Wilfrid J., and Massey, Frank J. *Introduction to Statistical Analysis.* 2d ed. New York: McGraw-Hill, Inc., 1957.

Downs, Anthony. *An Economic Theory of Democracy.* New York: Harper & Row, 1957.

————. *Inside Bureaucracy.* Boston: Little, Brown and Co., 1967.

Dunlop, John T. "The Task of Contemporary Wage Theory." In *New Concepts in Wage Determination,* edited by George W. Taylor and Frank C. Pierson. New York: McGraw-Hill, Inc., 1957, pp. 117–139.

Fenno, Richard F., Jr. *The Power of the Purse: Appropriations Politics in Congress.* Boston: Little, Brown and Co., 1966.

Festinger, Leon. "A Theory of Social Comparison Processes." In *Small Groups: Studies in Social Interaction,* edited by A. Paul Hare, Edgar F. Borgatta, and Robert F. Bales. New York: Alfred A. Knopf, Inc., 1955, pp. 163–186.

Garms, Walter I. "The Financial Characteristics and Problems of Large City School Districts." *Educational Administration Quarterly* 3 (1967): 14–27.

Gerwin, Donald. "Compensation Decisions in Public Organizations." *Industrial Relations* 8, no. 2 (February, 1969): 174–184.

————. "A Process Model of Budgeting in a Public School System." *Management Science.* In press.

————. "Towards a Theory of Public Budgetary Decision Making." *Administrative Science Quarterly.* In press.

Hatry, Harry P., and Cotton, John F. *Program Planning for State, County, City.* State-Local Finances Project. Washington, D.C.: The George Washington University, 1967.

Homans, George Caspar. *Social Behavior: Its Elementary Forms.* New York: Harcourt, Brace and World, Inc., 1961.

James, H. Thomas; Kelly, James A.; and Garms, Walter I. *Determinants of Educational Expenditures in Large Cities of the United States.* Stanford, Calif.: Stanford University, School of Education, 1966.

Lester, Richard A. *Economics of Labor.* 2d ed. New York: The Macmillan Co., 1964.

Lurie, Melvin. "The Growth of Fringe Benefits and the Meaning of Wage Setting by Wage Comparisons." *The Journal of Industrial Economics* 15 (1966): 16–25.

March, James G., and Simon, Herbert A. *Organizations.* New York: John Wiley & Sons, Inc., 1958.

Martin, Roscoe C.; Munger, Frank; Herman, Harold; Birkhead, Guthrie S.; Burkhead, Jesse; Kagi, Herbert M.; Welch, Lewis P.; and Wingfield, Clyde J. *Decisions in Syracuse.* Metropolitan Action Studies, no. 1. Bloomington, Ind.: Indiana University Press, 1961.

McKean, Roland N. *Public Spending.* New York: McGraw-Hill, Inc., 1968.

Miller, Rupert G. *Simultaneous Statistical Inference.* New York: McGraw-Hill, Inc., 1966.

Miner, Jerry. *Social and Economic Factors in Spending for Public Education.* The Economics and Politics of Public Education Series, no. 11. Syracuse, N.Y.: Syracuse University Press, 1965.

Moore, Charles G., and Weber, C. Edward. "A Comparison of the Planning of Sales by Two Department Store Buyers." In *Management Action: Models of Administrative Decision,* edited by C. Edward Weber and Gerald Peters. Scranton, Pa.: International Textbook Co. In press.

Musgrave, Richard A. *The Theory of Public Finance: A Study in Public Economy.* New York: McGraw-Hill, Inc., 1959.

National Education Association, Research Division. *Local School Boards: Status and Practices.* Educational Research Circular No. 6. Washington, D. C.: The Association, 1967.

————. *Salary Schedules, Classroom Teachers, Districts having 3,000 or More Pupils, 1962/63–1964/65.* Washington, D. C.: The Association, 1962–1964.

————. *Salary Schedules, Classroom Teachers, Urban Districts 100,000 and Over in Population, 1957/58–1961/62.* Washington, D. C.: The Association, 1957–1961.

————. *Selected Statistics of Local School Systems 1965/66.* Research Report 1967–R15. Washington, D. C.: The Association, 1967.

————. *Teachers Salary Schedules in 125 Urban School Districts over 100,000 in Population, 1954/55.* Washington, D. C.: The Association, 1954.

Naylor, Thomas H., and Finger, J. M. "Verification of Computer Simulation Models." *Management Science* 14 (1967): 92–101.

Nealey, Stanley M. "Pay and Benefit Preference." *Industrial Relations* 3 (1963): 17–28.

Patchen, Martin. *The Choice of Wage Comparisons.* Englewood Cliffs, N.J.: Prentice-Hall, Inc., 1961.

Pigors, Paul, and Myers, Charles A. *Personnel Administration.* 4th ed. New York: McGraw-Hill, Inc., 1961.

Pittsburgh Board of Public Education. "Combined Balance Sheet for the Month Ending August 31, Exhibit 'A.' " *Minutes of the Board of Public Education* 45 (1955/56)–54 (1964/65).

Pittsburgh Business Review. "Tables." 32 (1962)–34 (1964).

Rosenstengel, William Everett, and Eastmond, Jefferson N. *School*

Finance. New York: The Ronald Press Co., 1957.

Ross, Arthur M. "The External Wage Structure." In *New Concepts in Wage Determination,* edited by George W. Taylor and Frank C. Pierson. New York: McGraw-Hill, Inc., 1957, pp. 173–205.

————. *Trade Union Wage Policy.* Berkeley, Calif.: University of California Press, 1948.

Simon, Herbert A.; Smithburg, Donald W.; and Thompson, Victor A. *Public Administration.* New York: Alfred A. Knopf, Inc., 1950.

Smithies, Arthur. "Conceptual Framework for the Program Budget." In *Program Budgeting: Program Analysis and the Federal Budget,* edited by David Novick. Cambridge, Mass.: Harvard University Press, 1965, pp. 24–59.

Vaizey, John. *The Economics of Education.* London: Faber and Faber, Ltd., 1962.

Weber, Max. *The Theory of Social and Economic Organization.* 1st ed. New York: Oxford University Press, Inc., 1947.

Wildavsky, Aaron. *The Politics of the Budgetary Process.* Boston: Little, Brown and Co., 1964.

Wildman, Wesley A. "Collective Action by Public School Teachers." *Industrial and Labor Relations Review* 18 (1964): 3–19.

Index

165